2013
THE BEST MEN'S
STAGE MONOLOGUES

2013
THE BEST MEN'S
STAGE MONOLOGUES

Edited and with a Foreword
by Lawrence Harbison

MONOLOGUE AUDITION SERIES

SMITH AND KRAUS PUBLISHERS

ISBN: 1575258447/781575258447
ISSN 2329-2695
Library of Congress Control Number:

Typesetting and layout by Elizabeth E. Monteleone
Cover Design: Borderlands Press

A Smith and Kraus book
177 Lyme Road, Hanover, NH 03755
Editorial 603.643.6431 To Order 1.877-668-8680
www.smithandkraus.com

Printed in the United States of America

Contents

Here you will find a rich and varied selection of monologues for men from plays which were produced and/or published in the 2012-2013 theatrical season. Most are for younger performers (teens through 30s) but there are also some excellent pieces for older men as well. Some are comic (laughs), some are dramatic (generally, no laughs). Some are rather short, some are rather long. All represent the best in contemporary playwriting.

Several of the monologues are by playwrights whose work may be familiar to you, such as Don Nigro, Theresa Rebeck, Jeffrey Sweet, Nilo Cruz, Keith Reddin, Willliam Mastrosimone, Terrence McNally and Christopher Durang; others are by exciting up-and-comers such as Nicole Pandolfo, Adam Cunningham, Colman Domingo, Peter Sinn Nachtrieb, Ike Holter, Michael Rabe, Paul Downs Colaizzo and Greg Kalleres.

Many of the plays from which these monologues have been culled have been published and, hence, are readily available either from the publisher/licensor or from a theatrical book store such as the Drama Book Shop in New York. A few plays may not be published for a while, in which case contact the author or his agent to request a copy of the entire text of the play which contains the monologue which suits your fancy. Information on publishers/rights holders may be found in the Rights & Permissions section in the back of this anthology.

Break a leg in that audition! Knock 'em dead in class!

Lawrence Harbison
Brooklyn, NY

MONOLOGUES

Seriocomic
Tommy, twenties

Tommy tends bar at a go-go joint in New Jersey. He is talking to B.J., a local cop, who has observed that some of the women in the bar have been eyeing him. Tommy is not interested in them, which amazes B.J.

TOMMY: I've banged so many hot chicks it's ridiculous. I used to be in a band. MTV2 played our music video like on the hour the whole month of March 2009. We filmed the video ourselves. We did a major tour of New England. Played shows all up in Boston, Providence; even hit up some spots in Connecticut and Long Island. The Jersey Shore scene like mad. Then we started getting the Lower East Side spots, and then we started to really hit people's radar.

> *(He reminisces a moment.)*

That was so fucking awesome. Riding the wave of like, imminent success. One of the greatest feelings I've ever had. I scored so many chicks. So many hot chicks. Mostly NYU chicks in the city, but they're kinda worldly, you know, harder to impress. The chicks in New England, it was like, these chicks were dying for a taste of something bigger than what they could get at their local Stop and Shop, and to be banging a future potential rock star just set them off like a firecracker. I haven't gotten blown with that much enthusiasm since I was 15.

> *(beat)*

We were . . . we were so close. Came really close to getting a gig with EMI, Sony, Capital.

> *(beat)*

But fucking Darin. The lead singer. He just, he just couldn't not be a dick. It was like, he felt like finally, he was getting the recognition that was owed to him or some shit, so instead of being grateful for the opportunities he was more like, "fuck all of you for taking so long to notice."

(beat)

So he dicked around with Sony; free drinks, free food and then it was "more money or fuck you." Same story with EMI and Capital and even some smaller labels. And pretty soon our one video got old, our manager dropped us, and no one was left to finance any new songs or set up any new gigs.

(beat)

And here I am, not playing with a band, tending bar for what will be the 3rd year in a row. So if you wonder why I don't go ape over all the hot chicks in the bar, it's because I've fucked all the hot chicks already. And they liked me better when I was a rock star.

Information on this playwright may be found at:
www.smithandkraus.com.
Click on the AUTHORS tab.

Comic
Cecil, late thirties or Early forties, British.

*Cecil is the host of the TV talent competition America's
Brightest Star, and as part of the show he visits a small
town to audition the local librarian who is an aspiring
singer. While there he has sex with Amber, the librarian's
assistant with her own dreams of fame. After sex, Amber
asks him to rank her performance like he does with singers
on his TV show. He refuses initially, but after she says he's
afraid to tell her how good she was, he responds.*

CECIL: Initially, I found you attractive; at least, attractive
for this small town. Even though you dress country and
a little trashy, you know how to accentuate the positives.
More specifically, and I'm not trying to be rude, but you
were hiding your flaws in your legs and ass. And your tits
are saggier than I'd expect for someone of your age. That
will not bode well when you are older, like 26, 27. I ap-
preciate your eagerness in bed. One of the perks of my job
is digging for local talent on this show, local off-camera
talent, and you seemed to be the front runner. However,
I was quickly disappointed. I'm not trying to be rude,
but you kiss like a retarded monkey. Let me finish. You
were too passive, and your oral skills are just despicable.
Honestly, how are you going to get anywhere in life if
you can't give a decent blowjob? I was almost ready to
call it all off, but you gave off a vibe that you would really do anything, and I haven't had anal in a few weeks
and was feeling the itch. Imagine my disappointment
about that. Plus, you sort of squirmed and kept quiet…
when you weren't totally limp. Sex is like a dance, you
need to move and feel the rhythm. In conclusion, on a
scale of 1 to 10, 1 being my second wife's mother, and 10

being a threesome in Barcelona with Scarlet Johanssen and Penelope Cruz, I'd give you a 2 for oral, 3 for visual presentation, and a 3 for sexual performance, which averages out to a 2.67, but I'm willing to round up to 3. Because you're a nice girl. As for overall ranking, I'm sorry to say you wouldn't even crack the top 100. Not the worst, sweetie. Just . . . forgettable.

Seriocomic

Knox, a famous Edinburgh doctor, in his forties

Dr. Robert Knox, a famous surgeon and lecturer in anatomy in Edinburgh in the late 1820s, is speaking to his young assistant, William Ferguson, about Mary Patterson, a beautiful young prostitute that Ferguson has become involved with. Knox is warning the young man to stay away from all such entanglements. His career is built on dissecting bodies as he lectures, and he has been buying them from body snatchers and murderers, while pretending he believes they are legally obtained. He is also the husband of a lower class woman, and he has tried to harden his heart about the pleasures of the flesh and about love. He spends most of his time cutting open cadavers, and his interest here is in saving the career of his assistant, but he is also secretly a deeply troubled man whose cynicism will, in the course of the play, begin to crack as his morally questionable career begins to fall into ruins.

KNOX: There goes about the most remarkable specimen of perfectly formed young woman a man could ever hope to see. And she appears to have a level head on her shoulders as well. Extraordinarily attractive in every respect. Stay away from her. You must be strong. A man who finds himself in the power of a woman beneath his station deserves the hell he finds himself in. She's just what she says she is. She's a piece of flesh. An exquisite piece of flesh, a nearly perfect piece of flesh, from what I've seen. I'd be tempted to pay her price just to get a closer look at her anatomy. But that's all she is. Or at any rate, it's the only part of her you really care for. You wouldn't be at all interested in what was going on in her head if she wasn't walking around in a body like that, now, would you? She could have an intellect like Shakespeare and you wouldn't give her the time of day if she didn't happen to have the face and body of a goddess. And don't give me any rubbish about the beauty of her soul. She's got no more soul than a hog, or the moon. It's just a body you think you love, and the body rots. And hers will rot soon, given the life she leads. And then what will you have? A fat, ignorant, disease-ridden old whore. Try and love the soul in that. It is only your medical skills that I have much interest in, and they are potentially quite significant, but you cannot be a successful man of science if you continue to allow this infatuation to trouble your mind and hamper your studies. To frequent whores is a lamentable but minor vice. To become emotionally involved with one is very foolish. And I have no tolerance for fools. I hope we understand one another.

Information on this playwright may be found at:
www.smithandkraus.com.
Click on the AUTHORS tab.

ANATOMIES

Don Nigro

Dramatic

Knox, a famous Edinburgh doctor, in his forties

Dr. Robert Knox, a famous surgeon and lecturer in anat-
omy in Edinburgh in the late 1820s, is giving one of his
anatomy lectures, which are usually accompanied by the
dissection of a corpse, sometimes illegally obtained. He
has pretended not to notice that his fresh supply of corpses
has been increasingly obtained from body snatchers and
murderers, but the latest corpse, that of a beautiful young
prostitute, Mary, who has clearly been murdered, is ex-
tremely troubling for him, and he finds himself hesitant to
defile her body by cutting into it. He has become wealthy
and famous by hardening his heart, not being squeamish,
gazing cynically upon ideas about love and the beauties of
the flesh, but now he is beginning to crack, and his world
is starting to crumble. The tension in his soul is becoming
more and more visible in his lectures.

KNOX: The gentleman in the front row asks a very good
    question. He wonders why, in my most recent lectures,
    I speak more than I dissect. I must reveal to you a secret.
    The secret is that I, yes, even I, the legendary Dr. Robert
    Knox of Ten Surgeons Square, do have, at the core of
    my being, a certain revulsion for cutting into flesh. It
    comes and goes, but it's been uncharacteristically strong
    lately. I had every intention of dissecting a magnificent
    specimen of young womanhood for you today, but in
    the event I find that I am mysteriously disinclined to. I
    believe I am not prepared to share her with you yet. When
    one observes this creature, the perfection of her physical
    form, one is almost tempted to forget the festering bag
    of guts that rots inside her. But having seen the insides
    of countless others, one can't forget. What is hidden is

seldom beautiful, my friends. What is hidden is in fact seldom exceeded in terribleness by what we had feared, for at the core of things, we discover a universe which is even more rapacious and inhuman that we could have imagined in our worst nightmares. God observes his creation, watches it grow, becomes disenchanted with it, falls out of love with it, and in the final analysis kills it, then carefully observes the progress of its decomposition. For analysis kills, and decomposition is but the analysis of matter by God. It is a matter of some embarrassment to me that I find myself unwilling to violate the flesh of this loveliest of cadavers. I have grown weak, perhaps. I have grown a little foolish. I have succumbed to the beauty of a created object. This sort of attachment can only come to no good. For to succumb to the beauty of any living thing is to embrace a corpse. This is the true image of love, for even when the beloved is warm and alive, one is always embracing a skeleton, kissing the lips of the hideous grinning skull beneath the skin. There is only a thin layer of dying flesh between one's lips and the bony thing which is the head of the bag of festering guts one imagines one will love forever. So do not allow yourselves to be taken in by beauty, my friends. Beauty is a thin layer of paint which conceals corruption and death. Steel yourselves, gentlemen, or you will find yourself, on some dark night, making the beast with a skeleton. You are born into a charnel house. Do not be deceived by the terrible joke of love. And yet take note that still, knowing this, I cannot bring myself to violate her flesh. Thus endeth the sermon for the day. Go and think upon these mysteries.

Information on this playwright may be found at:
www.smithandkraus.com.
Click on the AUTHORS tab.

Seriocomic
Marcel, twenty-three

On the Quad on a brisk fall afternoon, a frazzled young man is being followed by a small stern girl, Beth Looper, 23, a brilliant student at Saddlewood College. She has romantic feelings for her friend, Marcel Staniciu 23. They are Romantic Literature majors. Here he confronts her and sets her straight.

MARCEL: Lower your voice. I was not playing with Elina Plugaru's ponytail during the lecture. I was not stroking it. I was barely petting it. It was just there. Dangling freely on my desk while I'm taking notes. What the hell am I supposed to do? Who are you to judge me? Why are you even watching me? Beth!? Beth. NO! NO! What do you even care what I do with Elina Plugaru's hair? You're not my girlfriend. You had your chance one year ago at Model Congress and you blew it, lady! And don't pretend you were drunk on wine coolers because the stuff you said was really cruel and small and unforgiveable. And it wasn't a perm—it was a relaxer. Many men use it. I told you—my cousin Manny mixed the ammonium thioglycolate with too much petroleum jelly and then left it in too long . . . and he should have used a neutralizer and just shut up. NO! Maybe I was just trying to look nice for you.
　　(pause)
That night at the Comfort Lodge was really important to me. It was supposed to have been special and it took a lot of planning on my part. I was very vulnerable and you knew it. It may not have been your first time but it was mine and I wanted it to be nice. And you ruined it. I had to borrow money from my Dad. I had to pay almost 300

dollars for a new ozonator because the rose petals got stuck in the filter of the jacuzzi. I had to borrow money from my Dad. Try lying to your Dad that you were at a Comfort Inn ALONE on a Tuesday night in a Jacuzzi filled with rose petals. He still won't look at me. It doesn't matter anymore. I'm happy now. Now finally I'm happy and I don't think about you anymore. I feel good about myself, and my hair is growing in, and I'm happy, and I aced my G.R.E.'s and now . . . NOW, you're acting like a scorned woman? Like you're Nastasya Filippovna from that stupid Dostoyevsky novel. If you think you're going to bring your jealousy and misplaced romantic aspirations into literary journal then you're dead wrong. You're not ruining my senior year, Beth.

Information on this playwright may be found at:
www.smithandkraus.com.
Click on the AUTHORS tab.

Dramatic
Thomas, thirties to forties

Thomas, an adult with the mind of a child, tells a dream he had to a social worker.

THOMAS: Well, I was sinking into the mud. It was sucking me down. I could hardly breathe. I was stuck there. Then down from the sky there came this sparkling bubble. And then the bubble popped and it turned right into a princess. And she was really really pretty. And she had a really pretty face. And she waved her wand. And it touched my nose. And the sky got all pretty colors. And white birds flew out. And all the mud disappeared. And I was standing there. And I was looking really clean. And I could do all these things with my arms. And so she said let's get married. And we got married and I was really really happy. So when I woke up I drew a picture of my beautiful princess and just stared and stared. And this is really weird: I kind of knew the face, even though I never saw it before. Do you think I ever really will find someone to marry me? I would be really really nice to her. All she would have to do is cook me meals two times a day or just one time and wipe my face really slowly. She wouldn't have to stay with me every minute. She could go out every night. She could gossip with her friends. I wouldn't care if she was a great big gossip. I would just want someone to be mine and that would be so nice. Why are you crying?

. *Information on this playwright may be found at:*
www.smithandkraus.com.
Click on the AUTHORS tab.

Lawrence Harbison

Dramatic
Thomas, thirties to forties

Art is a businessman who is visiting his wife in the mental ward. While making a business call, he allows Thomas to frisk him for lice, because he believes Thomas is a member of the staff. But Thomas is a patient, who misinterprets Art's words.

ART: *(into phone)* It's time to go for it. Take a good look. Closer. Really close. If you see any rough spots smooth them out now. Smooth them out or they'll rise up against you. They'll rise up, I'm telling you. Bob. Bob. Don't let them push you. You push them. Don't be afraid to press hard. Fiddle with 'em, you know? See if they jiggle a little. Let things get prickly. Make them sting. Keep looking for a break. Check out the terrain. If they give you an opening take it. There's bound to be a crack. Bob. Bob. Don't be afraid to get your hands dirty. Dig in. Pick away. Make your move before it gets messy. What? Go lower. Lower. Bob. I want you so low they're shaking. Let them shake. If they shake, lick them. Sure you can lick them. I'm not asking, I'm demanding: lick them now. I want you to swallow those guys right up. Chew them up and swallow them down. What are you waiting for? Are you afraid to use your god damn teeth? Devour them now. They're not going anywhere. If they hang in there, cut them off. Cut them right off—but no, don't touch those. Back off completely. Do a dance. That's right. Keep our butt covered. I don't want anything left hanging in the wind. Keep dancing. That's it. Yeah. Dance. Right. Later.

Information on this playwright may be found at:
www.smithandkraus.com.
Click on the AUTHORS tab.

THE ART ROOM
Billy Aronson

Dramatic
Thomas, thirties to forties

Thomas, a mental patient, has agreed to check Art, a visitor, for lice. In return, Art has agreed to listen to Thomas talk about his day. Though Art is making a business call, Thomas thinks he is instructing him.

THOMAS: My magical princess is on her way. I really really can't wait. When she gets here I'll be really really happy. I'm going to really tidy up and it's going to be really nice and really tidy. There are going to be pretty colors and she'll be really pretty and you should have seen her in my dream, she had a really pretty face and hands and pretty eyes and she was so pretty that I'm going to be so happy, think how happy, with those pretty hands and face, that's why everything's just got to be so bright and really pretty just for her. And since she's so really pretty she gets really pretty things all around her every single day. Anyway I saw her in a dream and I'm going to be so happy every little day now, every single little day, because she'll be oh so really nice to me all the time she'll be really nice. I can just feel her on the way, I can tell she's really coming because can't you just sometimes tell when something's about to happen, you know you can sometimes tell? So I have to get everything really neat and really pretty so I really have to go now bye bye bye.

Information on this playwright may be found at:
www.smithandkraus.com.
Click on the AUTHORS tab.

Dramatic
Rob, thirty

Speaking to the audience, Rob is defending the inappropriate relationship he has with his colleague's daughter, who is 24, but acts much younger and is emotionally challenged.

ROB: You know about me? How I used to be? Well, you'd hear it around Syosset. If you kept you're ears open you'd hear what they're saying about me. So what? I don't give a shit. I built that bike you know. Piece by piece. I bought the parts. I selected each one separately for quality. And I put it together. And it works and it gets me where I need to go. And I'm like a car but I'm the engine you know. I made the parts. The flesh and the steel and it all passed through my hands and I deserve some fucking respect for that shit. I don't get it. I'm not gonna be pushed around. No one is pushing me around. There is nothing soft. Nothing quiet about me, nothing small about me. You can't blame me. I don't know when the things I wanted became so hard. My parents they had a little house and some kids. They had a boat and a truck and a basketball net and camping on vacation and shit. And I'm just this asshole with a camera and a bike, riding around like a clown, a clown with very good posture but nonetheless, some asshole. And I'm not trying hurt no one. I just need what you need, alright? Give me a break! Just let me keep going. You don't see my plan okay. You don't see where this is heading. It's going somewhere it's all gonna be clear and no one's gonna be mad about any of it when they figure it out. Because I see far into the future Baby, I see what none of you seen yet. I see where we're going cuz I've been there and I'm going back bigger. And I'm taking what's mine this time. I'm not getting kicked around my nobody. I'm catching it all on tape. I got it locked down. Don't worry about it. You're gonna understand. You'll get it when we get there. You'll see.

Information on this playwright may be found at:
www.smithandkraus.com.
Click on the AUTHORS tab.

THE BAD GUYS
Alena Smith

Dramatic
Jesse, twenties

Jesse has dropped by to visit his old friend Noah before Noah heads out to Los Angeles to pursue his dream of becoming a film maker. Here, he rants to Noah and others in the back yard of Noah's mom's house.

JESSE: Fuckin' Chris. Thinks he's so great cause he's going back to school. Well, you know what that means? Debt. More debt. Chris and April are gonna be in debt for the rest of their lives, and so is their kid. And so are my parents. I'm the only one with my head above water, and that's because I sell ganja to children. But of course, that's a band-aid solution. Ultimately, I'm fucked too. This whole country's fucked, you know that? Thanks to people like Fink. You know Fink was the one who kept telling my dad to build those shitty spec houses! Oh, everyone's doing it. Easy money. Get in on the game, Glen. Cause houses aren't for living in anymore. They're for flipping! Like burgers. But then the big burger bubble blows up. And who do you think gets bailed out? Not us, nah. We go broke. Fink and his buddies—*they're* the ones getting government cheese. Welfare for Wall Street that's what America is all about. Ain't that ironic? Don'tcha think? Cause America, we hate welfare! Like when I see fat bitches with babies hanging off their tits lining up for a handout that just makes me *sick*. As an *American*, that just makes me puke a little bit in my mouth. But now Fink and his friends, they're special. They're too big to fail! So these guys, these banksters, what they need from us—what they need from *you*, America—is, oh, just a little thing called seven hundred billion dollars. Oh— and that's just to start. An appetizer—no, an appeteaser.

That's what they call it at Applebee's, right? And you know what they call it at KFC.

(Beat.)

A Double Down. Yup. That's what we did here, America. We just doubled the fuck *down* on this bullshit.

Information on this playwright may be found at:
www.smithandkraus.com.
Click on the AUTHORS tab.

Dramatic
Gary, twenties to thirties

> *Gary is a squatter, living in foreclosed houses until the*
> *bank auctions one and then moving on to the next one.*
> *He is somewhat demented, possibly dangerous. He is*
> *talking to Crystal, who lost her house and is now staying*
> *in another foreclosed house while she tries to get her life*
> *back together. She would hole up in a shelter and lost*
> *custody of her 5 year-old daughter, Bethany. Gary wants*
> *her to fight back.*

GARY: They're socializing her. They're teaching her not to
hit other kids, and to keep her skirt down, and raise her
hand when she has to go to the bathroom. Every single
thing her body wants to do is getting smashed down by
the military-industrial complex, and the worst part is that
it happens all day, every day, to everyone, and everyone
just lets it happen. Look at you: you go around all day
with that big, fake smile pasted across your face, selling
people a bunch of crap they don't need so you can go buy
crap *you* don't need. "I just *have* to make this sale." You
completely bought the government messages. But what
happens now? Are you gonna just curl up and die? Or are
you gonna fight back? Because when you have to struggle
for food and shelter, just like we did millions of years
ago, boom! You start getting your mind back. And we
have to take advantage of this time and fight the system
until we obliterate it. You and me, we'll never recover a
hundred percent; but your daughter's young; she might
still have a chance . . . You see, it won't be a collective
society anymore where technology controls the masses.
It'll just be individuals and small groups. And when the
centers of technology and finance go down, we need to

be ready to survive. Small, nomadic groups have the best shot at it. I know how to trap food and I know all the edible plants. I'll tell you what you should do. You pick her up from school. You say, "Don't worry, honey, we're never going back there again." Then the three of us get in your car and we start driving. We drive until we hit wilderness. Someplace without all this EMF radiation. We build a shelter. Or find one. And we've got the seeds of a new society. XX . . . XX . . . XY.

Dramatic
Klass, twenty-seven, African American

Klass is a homeless man who lives on a bench in a housing project. He has arranged various objects around him, to which he addresses this monologue. Klass evokes a performance style similar to that of Robert Preston's "Trouble" from The Music Man. *He also taps into a Baptist minister style a la Rev. BW Smith. If a middle ground can be found between these two, that'd be so so cool.*

KLASS: You may not be fully aware of the times we're livin in. The times that they don't print in our papers or splash across our screens or pump through our radios. I suggest you might not be aware because I see you. I watch you. I see you holding on to what little sanity and security you have left, squeezing it so tight that the color is leaving your fingers, draining from your hands. The squeezing is causing your muscles to ache. Jaws to clinch. And you think that pain is a sign of sanity? Security? It's not, my friends. It's not.

> *(Pause)*

There's a wind blowin through you.

> *(Pause)*

A violent gust of truth.

> *(Pause)*

It starts out as a breeze somewhere in here:

> *(Points at his heart.)*

and it wakes up all the noise inside of you. Then that breeze gets in your blood. Travels through every vein. Head to toe. It gathers enough speed to the point where it won't let you sleep at night. That breeze becomes a gust and that gust won't let you be still. Won't keep your troubles quiet. You sit on stoops, lean against cars, stand under the moon—restless. You walk to one end of your neighborhood then back to the other end, go sit back on that same stoop, sit under the sun—restless. The gust is stirring your soul. It's pulling up memories from way down deep, from the cracks and crevices covered with scabs and scars. We swallow what we think is liquor, inhale what we think is weed, inject what we think is freedom. We alter our state of reality so we don't have to participate in it. So we can't be responsible, aware, dependable. And what happens when we hear a scream? When we see someone who looks like us, cornered? Pleading? Hm?

(KLASS turns away as if he's ignoring a weeping soul.)

We cross the street. We turn the music up a little louder. We drink, smoke, squeeze . . . but we still hear it. It never goes away. The wind, the noise, that somebody pleading . . . it's not going away. And then the next somebody is cornered.

(KLASS turns away.)

And then the next one . . .

(He turns away.)

And then the next—until it's you. And then you want to know why no one's coming to save you, to take you to a safe place?

Bob: A Life In Five Acts
Peter Sinn Nachtrieb

Comic
Bob, twenties to thirties

Bob, Our Hero, believes he is destined for Great Things. Meanwhile, for now he lives at a highway rest stop.

BOB: I am going to be a hero for someone.
(BOB shows his list.)
My list of great ideas is growing longer and stronger every day. So much I can do and this is where it begins, Bob's diary. I can make this the greatest rest stop in the country. I'll clean the bathrooms every other hour. I'll carve better trails into the hills and tidy the bushes where the men meet their soul mates. Late at night, using paint left by the trash, I will reconfigure the parking design to foster a greater sense of community amongst the travelers. Bob, rest stop maverick. The Bob Memorial Rest Stop. Put it on a plaque. Do you think when someone reads your name on a plaque hundreds of years after you're dead, for a brief instant, you exist again? All of a sudden the patch of mushrooms, the bit of that tree, that soil or dust that were once your molecules suddenly experience a moment of connectedness, a memory of their past teamwork as being part of a human being that did something that was so important it had to be recognized. On a plaque.

Comic
Bob, twenties to thirties

Bob, the Incurable Optimist, has lost his optimism.

BOB: Are you listening, Barry Metcalf? Are you listening, Poncha Springs? I have a father, who lived hard, smelled rough, who has done some terrible things in his life and he's still a greater man than all of you! And somewhere in America I have a mother who has the power to curse through voicemails. Who had a beautiful Ringertraum. And I have her smile. And they've ruined their lives for me. You evil, selfish, despicable land. You eat my father, poison my Jeanine, steal my Amelia, and you have soiled every beautiful idea I've written on pieces of paper with your mediocre filth. YOU ARE KILLING EVERYTHING I LOVE! Well I curse you, Barry Metcalf. I curse Sioux Falls, Roanoke, and Aberdeen. I curse this ENTIRE NATION to live a life that befits who they are! No more fudge shops. No more lists. America does not deserve the love and passion of a dreamer. But I do. I have a dream. And I will pursue it by any means necessary until there is justice, until the pain you have inflicted upon me is avenged. I have a RINGERTRAUM and BOB WILL NOT BE STOPPED. Good luck, Bob. Good luck, indeed.

Dramatic
Nixon, fifty-four

It's 1967, and Richard Nixon is being pressured by his former campaign manager to run for president in 1968. He's tempted, particularly as Lyndon Johnson is vulnerable. He's not worried about Johnson, though—he's worried about his own party's elite, who have never liked him.

NIXON: You know the definition of a pussy? "Someone who's afraid of a Democrat." With what they've done on civil rights, the Democrats have lost the vote of every white person who isn't a tea-sipping tenured professor at Yale. Now the rich, the rich have always been Republican but we couldn't get the working man, the blue collar fellow, to see that the GOP was on his side. Now that the Democrats are sending buses full of the coloreds into white schools, believe me, we can have those blue collar votes. *Those* are people who have never felt above anyone *except the blacks. That was their one comfort:* we're down, we're down but at least we're above the fucking blacks. But now those buses are telling them that they are *the same* as the blacks. And that is a message those white voters do not want to hear. So mark my words: the candidate who identifies this grievance for the voters, who knows the right words to explain it—not the old slurs that are a stain on our past, but I mean, what I mean is: the words with the right resonance—that candidate could steal the South, and the larger white vote, from the Democrats for a generation. I'll *flay* the Democrats. I'm worried about *our* people. Not one of them stands a chance against Johnson. My fear is with the party elite, the boys behind the scenes. As you know, that crowd has never liked me. For a long time, the GOP was the Gentleman's Party and we never played rough. There was something in that old WASP establishment that said it was more important to fight fair than to win. Which is why we didn't win for 20 years. My point is: *Nixon is the one who stopped playing like that. Nixon's the one who said what's the point of fighting if not to win? Nixon's the one who said Helen Douglas was pink right down to her underwear.* I'm the one who did what it took, against her, against Voorhis, and because of it, Nixon's rise was meteoric. And the old Guard has always had it in for me because I wasn't one of them. I was *too pushy*. They don't want me and I found that out in a way that haunts me to this day. You know what I mean. Of all my crisis, it was the worst and the most applicable now. I think it holds everything we need to know about whether I can get back in and take this thing. Of course the Democrats have always hated Nixon, and they relish any chance to stick the sword in and twist it, along with their friends in the liberal Hebrew media. The dark secret of Checkers is that Nixon's enemies at the time, the people who came after Nixon with the knife, the people who sharpened the blade and grasped the handle and prepared to plunge it in, were Republicans.

Dramatic

Nixon, thirty-nine

Richard Nixon, the 1952 Vice Presidential candidate, has been accused of accepting money from rich businessmen for his personal use. Adlai Stevenson has a "slush fund" too—but the media have dismissed this as inconsequential, even as they hound Nixon. Eisenhower is being pressured by the party bosses to dump Nixon from the ticket. Nixon is being pressured to withdraw. Here he tells his campaign manager why he won't do it.

NIXON: That is typical of the way the sons-of-bitches in the media in this country work. It's always the same with the rich guys, the Ivy Leaguers—they get away with murder and those of us down here on the street, the ones who don't have a special "in," who are fighting and scrapping to get *the goddamn job done, we're always on fucking trial!* I'm sick of it! Remember when FDR was flying his dog Fala around on army planes? *Huge waste of money* and everybody just found it cute because it was FDR. We are a one-party country. The Democrats have the House, the Senate, the Supreme Court, they've had the presidency for 20 years and they own the lapdog liberal media. That's not the way it was intended. Well, my whole life's been based on three words: Let me in. All along people tried to block me. At Whittier they wouldn't let me in the fraternity that all the best football players were in. I was on the team but still they wouldn't let me in the club. So what did Nixon do? Accept it? Slink off? No, sir. I created my own club. I beat 'em, I beat 'em all. I don't quit, I never quit, and they'll only push me off this ticket over my goddamned dead body!

THE CHEKHOV DREAMS
John McKinney

Seriocomic
Eddie, late thirties

*Eddie, a rakish, devil-may-care bad boy, is speaking to
his younger brother Jeremy, a once-aspiring writer who
has succumbed to depression over the death of his fiancée three years ago. It is now New Year's Eve, and Eddie
has come to Jeremy's apartment with a resolution—to
get his brother to start socializing again, and, hopefully,
resume his writing. Jeremy resists, clinging to the safety
and numbness of sleeping all day and avoiding people as
much as possible. The argument escalates and for a very
brief moment the two brothers nearly come to blows. This
speech is what follows.*

EDDIE: Look at you! You're ready to fight me rather than
leave your fucking cryo-chamber here, even for a few
hours a week?! And you were going to lecture me on ad-
diction? Oh sure, sleep . . . it's perfectly legal, but buddy,
when you wake up your life will still be on pause. And
Kate will still be dead. Christ, you may not have been
in the car with her that night but you might as well have
been. The way you've been trashing your life these last
three years . . . Yeah. I know what you're thinking. The
difference is, when I waste my life, I do it in style. Take
this coke. This is Calvin Klein. Pharmaceutical grade
Peruvian with a few grams of Ketamine to take the edge
off. An addict wouldn't know the difference but I do.
Because I'm not an addict. I'm a connoisseur! I could
write a fuckin' guidebook on the hottest after hours clubs
. . . the best escort services. Which massage parlors give
"happy endings." Superficial people everywhere look up
to me because I make empty phrases sound profound.
It's true! I'm the poet laureate of small talk! Of course

it's all meaningless crap, I know that. And for me, that's fine. I don't want to know the meaning of life. What a fuckin' responsibility that would be. But you . . . you're not afraid to feel things, cut yourself open, feel around. Why, I have no idea. But if you have the courage to do that, and write about it honestly—I think a lot of other people would recognize those same, fucked up feelings in themselves. Don't you see? It's people like you who can explain all this crazy, scary shit to people like me, so when we're old and urinating on ourselves we can take solace in knowing that even ridiculous lives like mine actually meant something. You don't get that from a crack pipe; you get that from art. From books. To deprive the world of your gift the way you're doing now, now that is a wasted life.

Comic
Dusty, twenties to fifties

Dusty enters the bar limping to see Twinkles and Happy staring each other down, their guns on the table.

DUSTY: My cat died last week. Thirty-seven years old and died falling off the counter. She was dead before she hit the ground I suspect. I still haven't buried her. I'm too sad about it. I just stuffed her in the freezer and now whenever I want a popsicle, I see her and I start crying again. On top of that, yesterday, I was sitting on my couch and I noticed a tear in it. I should probably get some thread and stitch it up. It'll just get bigger if you don't do something about it. You know what they say, a stitch in time . . . something something. Something about stitches. But it applies universally. To all ways of fastening things. Like pull up your zipper now or you'll be cold later. Or take the antibiotics now before you give it to other people. Or like, go to rehab before you OD on cough syrup or PCP or whatever. Or like, take care of your mama. My mama's doing okay. In fact, I was having a pretty good day if I wasn't thinking about the cat or my couch. But then Shotgun shot me in the foot. I'll probably get gangrene. I'm hoping the burlesque show might cheer me up. Hey what are you guys doing?

Dramatic
Him, forties

Construction of the Human Heart *is a play about writing a play. The characters, a married couple, are writers. Here, the man speaks to his writing partner/wife.*

HIM: You look like a scene by Caryl Churchill. *Serious Money*. They bought a whole new kitchen because he got this new job. They went to Ikea. She must have told you. They've got serious money coming in now. He broke in. He got in. He got a job on a show about a hospital or cops, or maybe they're lawyers, I dunno, I don't remember but he's in. Horacio is in! And it's a TV show and it's TV money and so he bought a whole new TV kitchen—from Ikea. It's not freezing over there anymore. It's Scandinavian!—but it's heated. He didn't wanna tell me because about the job because he thought it would depress me. So—Karen told me. I can't believe she didn't tell you. She's your friend. She's your friend now—right? Right. Those people over there look happy. They're drinking champagne. They look very—satisfied. Wonder why they're drinking champagne. Wonder what they've got to be happy about? Wonder if things might work out better for us if we start to live in the present tense. That Ikea guy's the richest man in the universe . . . Richer than Bill Gates. And it's all in boxes. You put the things together yourself—out of little boxes. No craft, no art. Mass produced. Nobody likes the shit—but it's impossible to leave the place . . . If Bill Gates and the Ikea guy had sex and had a baby, it would be ugly and grey or wood paneled and laminated and you would have to assemble it yourself and it would be ultra-susceptible to viruses and it would die within two or three months of purchase. You would receive no refund, just a credit for a future birth or perhaps a replacement baby that has exactly the same built in defects and planned obsolescence as the last one. I used to be able to express anger. Now when people see me being angry; they laugh. They think I'm joking. I'm not. I'm not making a fucking joke. I am just—exhausted.

Information on this playwright may be found at:
www.smithandkraus.com.
Click on the AUTHORS tab.

Court-Martial At Fort Devens
Jeffrey Sweet

Dramatic
Rainey, forties

Julian Rainey, a middle-aged African-American lawyer affiliated with the Boston chapter of the NAACP, is defending two young African-American WACs in 1945. The two young women have been charged as a result of an incident in which a white officer, Colonel Kimball, insulted them by calling them "black" at a time when the term was considered an insult. The young women, responding to this insult, refused to return to duty and are being court-martialed for desertion, a very serious offense during time of war. In his summation, Rainey connects their protest to the larger context of racial issues in the army in World War II. The Lieutenant Stoney to whom Rainey refers is a female African-American officer Rainey put on the stand to make vivid the pull between her duty and her sense of outrage regarding Kimball's behavior.

RAINEY: I would like to read something that appeared in the paper under the headline: "Negroes, Whites Fight Side by Side for U.S." This is dated Paris, March 19. "Negroes and whites are now fighting shoulder to shoulder in the same outfits in both the First and Seventh Armies, marking a break in the U.S. Army's traditional policy of segregation. So reported the Army newspaper *Stars and Stripes* today from the First Army Front. Negro platoons have been assigned to rifle companies of infantry divisions in both armies in response to repeated requests from the Negroes themselves for a chance to fight for their country." America, of course, is the only country among the Allied forces that segregates soldiers because of color. England doesn't, and in the colonies the colored soldiers go in with the rest. In Canada they go in with the rest, and in all the other countries there is no distinction. These young women chose to come into the Army. They chose on the basis of the promise that was made as to the training that they would get. They came in on that promise, and that promise was simply taken away from them by an officer who did not like to see them in white uniforms. We are fighting for the unconditional surrender of those who discriminate against men and women because of color or creed. That is what we are fighting for. That is what they enlisted to fight for. They had every right to expect that someone who embraces racism would wear the uniform of the enemy. Now, I put Lieutenant Stoney on the stand. I did so mindful of the discomfort of her situation. She is a conscientious, disciplined officer with a genuine respect for the chain of command. The questions I asked her were not intended to cause her distress, but to convey to you the dismay she felt on that day. Why is this relevant? An officer is supposed to inspire those who serve under him. To inspire, not to visit upon them humiliation and insult. The lieutenant testified she allowed no tears to go down her face. If that is so, then I confess she has more fortitude than I would have been able to manage had I been in her place. Tears of rage are appropriate when a colonel in this army says, "We don't want any of you blacks taking temperatures. We don't want any of you blacks drawing blood. We don't want any of you blacks in the motor pool." When an officer puts on a uniform, he no longer has the luxury of representing just himself. He has the responsibility of embodying the ideals of the country that lends him the privilege of that uniform. Keeping in mind what you have heard in sworn testimony, are you prepared to affirm that Colonel Kimball embodies this country's values? Is he fit to be seen as representative of the United States of America? For that is the conclusion the world will draw, must draw if you punish these young women for their courage in standing up to him.

Seriocomic
David Jr., twenty-two

David Jr. is fresh out of college. He tells his parents what
he wants to do with his life. He wants to do something so
meaningful that it will get him on "Charlie Rose."

DAVID JR.: I don't want a job just for the sake of having a
job. I want to make a difference somewhere in the world.
I want my life to have meaning. Like, I was watching
that show 'Charlie Rose,' and this guy was on it who had
built some schools or something in India? No. Someplace
more topical. Afghanistan or something. There were all
these pictures of him with these school kids in burkas—
or, not the whole burka, but, you know, they looked
Middle Eastern. Whatever, the point is that I want to be
on *Charlie Rose*. I want to live the kind of life that people
want to interview you about. You know, it's like, you're
at a cocktail party somewhere wearing some traditional
piece of clothing from whatever country you're helping
and you're talking to some douchebag in a suit and he's
like, yeah, I just made blankity-blank amount of money
with a hedge fund, what do you do? And you're like: "I
just built a hospital in Bangladesh dickhead." Bam! You
win. And the guy realizes that that he's been wasting his
life. I don't know, maybe he suddenly wants to give all
his money to your hospital. That's how you make con-
nections. Networking. I mean, at the end of your life
you're going to ask yourself: "Did I make a difference?
Did I make some children smile?" Answer: Yes. I did. I
built a school somewhere. Not here, but in a place where
kids actually *like* going to school. I was on *Charlie Rose*.
Then you can die happy. Make people cry. All those
foreign kids who actually *like* going to school bawling

their eyes out. Because now that I'm dead who's going to help them? No one. They're screwed.

Information on this playwright may be found at:
www.smithandkraus.com.
Click on the AUTHORS tab.

Dramatic
Eugene, early twenties

Eugene Freer, a young midwestern U. S. Navy veteran, has just completed his military service and returns home to his wife, EMILY. EUGENE's aberrant behavior is disturbing to EMILY and his best friend LEO, particularly when EUGENE spends an increasing amount of time in the bathroom with a metal lunchbox he keeps locked and by his side at all times. This searing exploration of male military sexual trauma reveals a facet of military life rarely unveiled to the public.

Note: After his suicide attempt with a broken Shasta Root Beer bottle, Eugene is hospitalized in the psychiatric ward of a VA Hospital. Following his assault on another patient, EUGENE finally unburdens himself to his psychiatrist and explains the ritual of Crossing the Line.

EUGENE: They do it in the Navy when the ship crosses the line . . . the equator. It's some tradition . . . supposed to make men out of us . . . loyal to each other . . . Fella told me it goes back hundreds of years . . . sailors do it all over the world. See, guys who already crossed the equator, they're Shellbacks, sons of King Neptune. Us guys who never crossed the equator, we were slimy Pollywogs . . . One guy dressed up like King Neptune, beard and all . . . he held that pitchfork thing . . . Then Davy Jones. . . not that short English guy who sang with the Monkees . . . another Davy Jones . . . something to do with the ocean, okay? During training, some guys started talking about it . . . said some Wogs—that's short for Pollywogs—got beat up so bad, they landed in the hospital . . . some drowned . . . became shark shit.

(Begins crying.)
I didn't sign up to die. All I wanted to do was keep up my mortgage payments. What does this have to do with proudly serving America? I got real nervous, but how you gonna back out once you're aboard, huh? Jump off? You're shark shit either way.

(He is starting to become agitated.)
Give me a minute. Lemme just get myself together here. Some older fellas said everything got changed back maybe 1991 when some Secretary of the Navy issued new instructions about that stuff. There was this meeting in Las Vegas where lots of girls got assaulted—you know—sexually, I mean—by Navy guys—officers—not enlisted men, okay? So I guess this Secretary guy said these rituals were okay to make good leaders out of us, help us respect each other. But the Navy wasn't supposed to do anything to embarrass or hurt anyone. Until it started and I realized whatever stupid-ass instruction he issued was all a crock of horseshit. You think some big-deal secretary knows what happens on a ship in the middle of the ocean? Or cares? Shit-fucking-no. He's in his fancy office inside some marble building in Washington that never leaks when it rains. While some asshole politician was signing more instructions and proclamations to get himself on the news, the Shellbacks were forcing us to dress up in women's clothes for a Beauty Bitch Contest. I could stand shaving cream and sticking my face into a toilet and eating garbage off the stomach of Neptune's baby, if that's all they were going to do. How the fuck do eggs squished into your hair and licking disgusting things off somebody's dirty feet make you a better sailor, huh?

Information on this playwright may be found at:
www.smithandkraus.com.
Click on the AUTHORS tab.

Dramatic
Eugene, early twenties

*EUGENE FREER, a young Midwestern U.S. Navy veteran,
has just completed his military service and returns home
to his wife, EMILY. EUGENE's aberrant behavior is disturbing to EMILY and his best friend LEO, particularly
when EUGENE spends an increasing amount of time in
the bathroom with a metal lunchbox he keeps locked and
by his side at all times. This searing exploration of male
military sexual trauma reveals a facet of military life rarely
unveiled to the public.*

*Note: Eugene is hospitalized in the psychiatric ward of a
VA Hospital. Eugene attacks a patient who makes homo-
sexual advances. Eugene finally explains to his psychiatrist
what happened on his ship during the Crossing the Line
ritual.*

EUGENE: They locked us in coffins of salt water. Felt like
I couldn't breathe. I never did learn to swim that good
in the few weeks they gave me to learn. They made us
strip naked and do the elephant walk. That meant we
had to parade around in a line grabbing onto the private
parts of the Wog in front of us, while the Wog behind
was doing the same thing to me, like elephants walk
trunk-to-tail. Everyone was watching and laughing at us,
hundreds of people. Girls, too. Then they told us to drop
to our hands and knees for the butt bite. So we crawled
around on deck, in a long line. I had to put my nose in
the asshole of the guy in front of me, biting on his butt,
while the Wog behind did it to me. You gotta bite and get
bitten hard enough to draw blood. After that, they tested
our ability to stand pain. They beat us. With red rubber

hoses. Hard, too. Some Shellbacks poured something on Wogs' butts first so it would burn our skin when we got hit. The Shellbacks really got out of control. They started shoving mop handles up inside us, back and forth, in and out, over and over, over and over, over and over. Four or five guys held me down so I couldn't get away. I asked them to stop it stop it stop it, but they just laughed and did it more more more more. It hurt, it hurt more than getting beat with the hose, even with that burning stuff poured on my skin. I begged them, "Please no more, no more no more no more no more no more," but the more I yelled, the more they laughed and kept going. Some officers did it to us, too. There was no one to help me, no one, no one. I hollered for them to stop it stop it stop it stop it stop it stop it, no more no more no more no more no more, but they wouldn't listen to me. I started to cry; couldn't help it. They called me a pussy. A Wog who couldn't take it like a man. Then I felt the first guy shoving his dick into my ass while the other guys held me down. It hurt worse than the mop handle. When he was done, another guy took his place, then another. I tried to get away, but they held me down. I looked around, saw the same thing happening to other guys. I threw up and then, I think I passed out, face down right in the pile of puke. Next day, my face was crusty with dry chunks of puked up garbage glued to it. I was so sore, I could hardly walk.

Information on this playwright may be found at:
www.smithandkraus.com.
Click on the AUTHORS tab.

Dark Radio
Colin McKenna

Ron, forties to fifties
Dramatic

Ron tells his son Tex about a radio show he heard.

RON: I was listening to this show on the radio. A scientific show. It was fascinating stuff. Deep in the Amazonian jungle they are finding great cities covered in megafauna and forgotten for a thousand years. They even found the remains of two mountain states high in the Andes, rows of crumbling pyramids hugging the desolate wind-ravaged slopes and grand monuments perched on top of barely accessible peaks—and this was not a bunch of savages jumping up and down in front of the campfire, they were massive civilizations, maybe over a hundred thousand souls, with complicated social structures, they created massive earthworks on the floodplain (that until recently researchers thought had been molded by Mother Nature not by primitive man), they had an alphabet before the Phoenicians, the concept of zero before the Babylonians—a thousand years ago this was the most advanced civilization of the face of the planet and by the time Columbus landed it had ceased to exist. What happened? Where did they go? How did they suddenly disappear in a historical blink? The scientists don't have an answer for that, only guesses: drought, war, disease, ecological disaster . . . a mini ice age. Whatever it was it was swift and deadly, the histories founded etched on the walls of the ruins suddenly stop with no warnings of impending doom, like a switch is flipped and a culture that rivaled ancient Greece goes dark. Then the jungle swallows what is left behind. Poof. Screw global warming, worry about the next ice age. It's coming. It's always coming. Mother Earth likes it cold. Most of her life she has preferred to wear a cloak of ice. Geophysicists regard warm periods like our present one, called the Holocene, as the exception to the rule. When she is ready for a deep clean, Mother Earth will scrape us and all that we have built from her face with tides of solid ice. This is not doomsday talk, it is a scientific certainty. The ground shifts beneath our feet. Nature will eventually win. There is no America, there is no human race, our history a brief momentary struggle lasting a geological nano-second. Nothing is secured, nothing is safe. Eventually the rain will breach the roof, the forest will rise again and pull down these walls, weeds will chew through the sidewalk. A cheap prefab McMansion like this maybe lasts 50 years without any upkeep. The chimney will last the longest but eventually that too will crumble and return to the dust.

Information on this playwright may be found at:
www.smithandkraus.com.
Click on the AUTHORS tab.

DEAD ACCOUNTS
Theresa Rebeck

Comic
Jack, late thirties

*Jack has mysteriously fled New York and shown up in Cin-
cinnati, in the house he grew up in. Here he is talking to
his sister Lorna about the food in NYC and how it doesn't
compare to a good ol' Cincinnati cheese coney.*

JACK: Right? I mean, precisely. I mean, it's, you know, in
New York, people eat like, you can go to a deli, or some
vendor on a street corner and it's all right, you know,
that's not bad, for just like food that you need to eat fast
to keep yourself going for the next ten hours. You can
do that there. Or, you go to some place like just some—
places that are, the food is incredible in New York. Steaks
that you can't, there is no, there are steaks that I have
eaten that I dream about to this day, that I ate, in New
York. Italian restaurants in New York are better than
Italian restaurants anywhere else in the world, including
Italy. And I do not say that lightly. I'm not talking about
pussy food. I'm talking about meals that go on for hours,
or days. One time I went to a dinner party, you had to
walk down three flights of stairs—I'm talking down,
into the earth, on subterranean passageways under a
lake, past an underground forest—no, I'm shitting you
about the lake and the forest but seriously, you had to
go down these stairs and through the kitchen and into
a like hidden room down there, used to be a speakeasy,
and then it was a wine cellar and now it's like this hidden
room and there was a dinner party, down there, under the
city, duck breast on a red wine reduction with shallots
and fennel confit, the thing was, plus someone stood up
and sang opera, seriously, one of the people at this dinner party was a guest artist with the Met or something

and he stood up and sang this fucking Puccini aria, the waiters were hovering by the doors to listen, the whole earth was silent. That's the kind of thing that happens around food, in New York. And it doesn't come close to a cheese coney. It just doesn't.

Information on this playwright may be found at:
www.smithandkraus.com.
Click on the AUTHORS tab.

Seriocomic
Jack, late thirties

Jack has mysteriously fled New York and shown up in Cincinnati, where he grew up. Here, he is talking to his sister Lorna about his wife and her snooty family.

JACK: Listen, check this out. Check this out. She's old money. She's old everything. You don't notice it right away, because she's so young and beautiful, but everything else is old. Her mother's wedding dress. They remake it every time someone gets married, so that your wife still looks hot in it, but it's old. Dad's apartment? Old. The house in East Hampton. Old. The family itself is so fucking old they're older than America. This is true. They are so old, that they have relics. From England. Yes. Relics. And one of these relics, is a tea pot. Yeah, like a silver tea pot. From England. It came over with them on the Mayflower. It is a Mayflower teapot. Yes. And this Mayflower teapot was given to me and my bride on our wedding day. It was our present. It was my welcome to the family present. So we're dividing the property, right? And things are—shit, they're, she's—it's, so I say, you know what? If it's going to be like this? You're going after me like this? Communal property, no prenup, no marriage, everything just gone, like worse than gone, like you have to punish me for ever thinking, fuck you, then that fucking teapot is part of the communal property. Right? The Mayflower teapot, that belongs to both of us! They gave it, to both of us! Only check this out. No one knows where it is. It's been in the vault, right, at the bank, since the wedding? It's just not there anymore. It's just gone. Mysteriously. Out of the BANK. Now, things disappear from banks. Nobody knows that better than me, how that can happen. But not a Mayflower teapot.

Information on this playwright may be found at:
www.smithandkraus.com.
Click on the AUTHORS tab.

Dramatic
Troy, twenty

Troy, a local, is Anne's boyfriend and plays in a local rock band. Troy and Anne overhear a fight between Laura, Anne's mother, and other family members. When Laura discovers Anne and Troy hiding, she treats them rudely before stalking out of the room. Anne is deeply embarrassed, but Troy shrugs it off.

TROY: Hey, it doesn't matter. I mean, . . . nothing matters. The world's totally fucked. The ocean's full of garbage, but we still eat the fish, right? Last summer my friend, Mitchell, he's at this party with his girlfriend and suddenly she says she wants to break up. Well, Mitchell freaks, can't believe it. He's super upset. Does a shit load of drugs, gets totally ripped, and on the way home he flies through a stop sign and nails this other car. Mitchell's dead. The couple in the other car is dead. It was the front page story in the *Star*. Pictures of the cars all wrecked and twisted. It was serious. But after the funeral I'm talkin' to his girlfriend, and she's a mess. And she tells me, she didn't want to break-up, but he wasn't paying enough attention to her, so she wanted to get a rise out of him.

    (slight pause)

People suck. That's the way it is. One day your girlfriend says, "I'm sorry if this ruins your life or anything, but I wanna to fuck this other guy now. See ya." And a couple months later that guy's gonna decide he wants to hook up with some other girl, and so on.

    (slight pause)

Your mom's been screwed by this guy, so she's got to take it out on someone. Me, I'm nobody, so she's a bitch to me. It's no big deal. I'll live. Hey, in some places people shoot each other over who can pray louder. So don't worry about this here.

Information on this playwright may be found at:
www.smithandkraus.com.
Click on the AUTHORS tab.

THE FALLEN
Yasmine Beverly Rana

Dramatic
Andrej, early twenties

Time: 1992
Setting: Kalinovik, Bosnia
A former school building used for the detention and systematic rape of Bosnian Muslim women for the purpose of ethnic cleansing.

Andrej, a 19-year-old White Eagle Militia member speaks to Kalinovik prisoner Mirela, a 19-year-old Bosnian Muslim woman.

ANDREJ: Do you want to kill me? I bet you do. I bet if I turned around and unchained you and if you grabbed my gun, you'd shoot me, not once, but several times, over and over again, until you were sure I was dead. Right? So that's why I'm not . . . letting you go. Not to punish you, but protect myself. This is not about you, but I have to watch out for myself. You could kill me. You want to, right? Say something. Say something so I know you're alive. I have to keep you alive for the next guy. (*Laughs*) Or else I get in trouble, and I don't want to get into trouble. I don't need any trouble. (*Beat*) Aren't you sick of this? I am. I don't even think you're pretty or anything like that. You're not my type. You're not ugly, you're just . . . someone I'd never notice. (*Beat*) No, I would notice. I would, because you're nice. I think you are . . . I really don't know you. You won't talk to me, but I can guess, yeah? I know you hate me. I hate myself, kind of. But this is not really my fault, you know. I didn't start this! Look at yourself for that! Yeah . . . well, I don't know anything. I just . . . I just go along with it all, you know?

(Beat) No, wait, you . . . you're okay looking. Pretty, a little. Say something. I don't want to hurt you, but I need you to speak. I don't even know what your voice sounds like. Maybe you lost it. Maybe you can't speak anymore. Then that's okay. Then I know . . . it's not because of me, just me. I won't be hurt. *(Quietly distraught)* I never hurt anyone before this. I never did. I would never have done anything . . . like this! Like this? Whatever this is . . . I still don't understand it, but I was never good enough at school to understand anything. So I never asked about anything. It's not like I didn't care . . . it was more like . . . why should I care? Did you care? I think you did. You're looking into the distance and I don't even know what you're looking at. What is it? A hole in the wall? A fly? Air? Whatever air looks like. What does it like? I don't know. *(Chuckles)* I don't even want kids. I don't even know you. Why would I want a kid with you? This makes no sense. I don't get it. I wish you could explain this to me, because I'm lost, right now. *(Beat)* But I always was. I don't know where I am. But you know where we are. You're very aware of where we are and what this is.

Information on this playwright may be found at:
www.smithandkraus.com.
Click on the AUTHORS tab.

Seriocomic
Sean, twenties

Sean tells his roommate Tom about how his dog died.

SEAN: Did I ever tell you about my dog Polo? My dog that drowned? His ashes are in my room. It was fucking awful. He disappeared one day. My baby-sitter picked me up and she's looking all serious, all ominous, "Sean, Polonius ran away." She's all Polo ran away. So I make all these signs, go searching every day. This is right in the middle of winter so it is cold as fuck and I'm walking around town hanging flyers all day asking, "Have you seen my dog Polonius, he'll come to Polo, he really likes cheese." Me and my dad race off to responses to the flyers all winter. And then springtime, it's all green and warm and shit, my mom picks me up from school and, "Seany, we found Polo." I'm all excited feeling like all my effort was worth something . . . He fell through the ice in the pool and when it melted he floated up to the top. I must have walked right by him a hundred times calling his name as loud as I could. I felt like such a dickhead. He was a great dog. I liked him more than I like you. But he's dead and you're not.

Seriocomic
Florimo, late twenties-early thirties

We are at the opening night of Vincenzo Bellini's I Puritani.
*Florimo, Bellini's lover, is talking to him about the day
Bellini composed the opera. "The Malibran" is a famous,
temperamental soprano.*

FLORIMO: I remember the morning you composed it. We
were in a villa overlooking Lake Como that one of your
admirers had lent you. There were birds sweeping back
and forth, back and forth over the lake, waiting to dive
down and snatch up some unsuspecting fish in an act of
necessity that seemed like random violence to someone
lying in bed watching them through open French doors
and you at an ill-tuned piano in a terrible mood composing this very music while hung-over from the night
before. We'd drunk only champagne. Someone had told
us that if we drank only champagne we wouldn't have a
hang-over but if we mixed the champagne with even a sip
of anything else, all bets were off. It was the Malibran.
She would know. She is the mistress of debauchery. I
made sure I drank only champagne that evening—you,
too, my love—and we drank it copiously. I was delighted
to prove her right. We got wondrously loaded. We sang,
we danced, we broke furniture, we peed off the balcony
and jeered at the moon. We toasted the Malibran again
and again for the gift of intoxication without remorse.
What a tumultuous, fucked-up drunken night. Suddenly
somehow it was the next morning. I don't think I've ever
woken up with a worse headache. When I challenged the
Malibran, she said obviously we hadn't been drinking
French champagne. All other champagnes gave you a
hang-over. Only French champagne didn't. I told her

she was full of shit and—if not shit—of herself—and maybe they were the same thing. She said, "Of course I am but you're the only person who would dare to tell me so." I don't think your friends and colleagues know what to make of me. I'm not an artist. I don't create. I can't do what you do. They think I keep your bed warm when no one else is in it. That's not even the half of it. I remember lying there that morning, looking at you across the room, barefoot in your nightshirt, hair crazy and uncombed, bent over the keyboard, hollow-eyed, beautiful, beautiful to me, oblivious to me, me watching you do what you do and falling in love with you all over again. I got aroused. I wanted to call you back to bed but I knew better. Besides, you wouldn't have heard me. And then suddenly you were finished and you looked over at me still lying in bed and you said, "It's done. I think it might be all right. May I play it for you?" You were like a little boy and you began to play this same music and sing in your own, almost truly-awful voice. No one sings Bellini like you, certainly they don't—even if they are the four greatest voices in the world. The world has the Puritans Quartet, I had Bellini himself. I was present at the creation. I was your world premiere. The Malibrans, the Grisis, the Rubinis can't take that away from me. I heard it first. It was beautiful. We both knew it

Information on this playwright may be found at:
www.smithandkraus.com.
Click on the AUTHORS tab.

THE GOLDEN AGE
Terrence McNally

Seriocomic
Bellini, thirty-three

Vincenzo Bellini, the composer of the opera I Puritani, *is back stage during the opening night performance, talking to some singers while they wait to go back on.*

BELLINI: "Write us a comedy." They don't take me seriously. They take my music very seriously but not me. "Write us a comedy." I want to write *The Puritans*. Yes, it's a ridiculous libretto but my music isn't. "Write us a comedy." Never "How can we serve you? What do you want to write, maestro?" The next time it will be the opera I want to write. There will be no literal-minded poet to drag me down with a pedestrian libretto. There will be no egos to satisfy but my own, which is so enormous it frightens me. No singers to flatter by composing to their strengths. Rubini wants high notes, Grisi wants mad scenes. I have become their slave and it's driving me mad. I hate mad scenes. People don't go mad because of a broken heart. They take to their rooms and weep in utter solitude. There is no cause for high notes when your heart is broken. The very lowest reaches of the voice are what are called for. I shall write a mad scene for Lablache. A mad scene for a bass! That would be a little more like it. Rossini thinks he wrote one in *Semiramis* but it was a shallow exercise in note spinning. People thought it was original because no one had done it before. That's a narrow definition of originality. I will give Lablache a mad scene in *Lear* that will terrify him. He will be frightened to sing it. He'll be unable to. The highest art should be un-performable. My masterpiece will be an opera that cannot be performed.

What they call art is artifice. No, what I call art is as free, as wild, as unmanageable as life itself. Away with structure. Only feeling matters.

Information on this playwright may be found at:
www.smithandkraus.com.
Click on the AUTHORS tab.

GREAT WALL STORY
Lloyd Suh

Dramatic
Stevens, mid to late twenties

Al Stevens, a reporter for a Denver newspaper in the late 1890s, has concocted with two other reporters a bogus story about the Great Wall of China being demolished, which has led to dramatic and tragic events in China. Here, he tells Harriet, who works for Joseph Pulitzer, that it was all a lie,

STEVENS: It's all lies, Harry! Great Wall story's just a big fat lie, every word of it, and I knew it from the get-go. I knew there wadn't no boat, there weren't no demolition men and they weren't from Colorado. But I printed it anyway, and now look. Read the trail of newsprint and you can see it—there's boats and boats in the Pacific on their merry way to save some souls, but keep reading, Harry, look at this, four weeks ago, the *Post*, violence in Shandung or Tung or whatever, Chinese peasants riot against some German Catholics, two weeks ago, wait where is it, here, okay, the *News*, Tsung what is that? Tsung lee Yah I can't pronounce that, but these government guys have words with the Kaiser, a missionary building burnt down in Tungchow. They went over there thinkin a wall was falling, but it never was and I knew it. I spread the lie and spread it some more, and I can't undo that. A week ago, the *Post* again, protests outside the Palace, pressure on the Empress Dowager, it's unrest, and three days ago the Reverend Sidney Brooks in a wheelbarrow, decapitated head in a muddy gully. Today, a list of names. Missionaries. Gone to some imaginary wall-free China only to end up losing their damn heads. We did this. We said their wall was comin' down and they started taking us down instead, who can blame 'em? When I was ten years old comin' home with my dad from hunting, there was this dirty old beggar standing on our front porch. He wasn't robbin' us, maybe he wanted to but he hadn't done a thing yet. But the possibility of a threat and guess what, my dad shot him dead in front of my eyes.

Information on this playwright may be found at:
www.smithandkraus.com.
Click on the AUTHORS tab.

Seriocomic
Taylor, thirties

Taylor has come to Molly's apartment holding a lamp which had been hanging in a coffee shop over a table where Taylor had seen Molly sit. Molly stopped going to the coffee shop, which prompted Taylor to tear the lamp from the ceiling and, screwing up the courage, knock on her door. He is standing there, holding the lamp as Molly answers. This is their first time meeting.

TAYLOR: It doesn't look right. This. This here. This light. It doesn't make any sense. Over a table. Without you there. And so, I sat there, in the coffee shop, looking at other people, being touched by the light. And I was . . . . sad. I sit there at 11:32 every day. And I leave at 1:01 every day. I take a long lunch. It takes me awhile to eat a muffin. And you arrive between 11:43 and 11:52. You get a coffee. You sit under this light. The same light. I saw you sit there. Four days in a row. Most people don't sit. They leave. But you sit. Somehow at the same table. Under the same light. And when the light shines on other people. Nothing happens. Yes. It doesn't work. It's not right. You haven't been there for three days. And. And. You have a table. May I stand on it? I am not an electrician. I'm a phenomenologist. It's like an electrician. Sort of. I mean. I believe if you peel away structures: words, conversations, the way we're told to behave, all of it. I believe there is essence underneath. Codes. We're being coded. So, you peel away the codes. Find the essence. But then, if you peel away the essence there are more structures.

   (Beat)

I'm not supposed to steal lights, you know. No one stopped me. I don't know why. I know the manager was looking. He has a beard that he colors. He is losing hair but keeps his hair in a ponytail, pulling more hair off of his head. He has a wart on his nose, and a laugh that is very loud and I think people like to hear his laugh. He wasn't laughing when I took this light. So.

(Beat)

I think he called the police. But. I didn't see any police so I came right here because I followed you once so I know you lived here. I wanted to say something to you but I couldn't say anything because the words wouldn't make sense and I needed to give you something so this is it. Because, that's the thing with words. If you peel those away, there is more essence. It continues. At the bottom is something outside of discourse. Words, I mean. There is something we can know, I mean. Can't know. Something we can't know. But it doesn't mean it isn't there. And. When you were under the light. I felt like the answer was somehow closer.

Information on this playwright may be found at:
www.smithandkraus.com.
Click on the AUTHORS tab.

HIT THE WALL
Ike Holter

Dramatic
Carson, twenties to thirties, African American

CARSON: Look upon me. Behold a true-blue bitch through
and through. Look upon one who has seen the end and
cross yourselves in fear of the eternal damnation and re-
percussanial happenstance that awaits the fate of the fakes
who try to put me in my place, Lookuponmemother-
fucker. I. Know. You. *Well.* You, black-thing, tight-tank-
top, mandingo. You, Guido, Latino, *el stupido* bottom,
bottom feeder, Never met a dick you couldn't lick, Never
met a dick you didn't like, I know your type, Creeping
like a cockroach in the night out of mind out of sight
cause y'all sissies *just don't look right* in the light, *Hell*
I've seen better bitches uptown at the dog pound before
the city puts em down, You mouth-breathing pimple-
popping pot-pushing no-dicked hypocrites, get off my
stoop get out my park and go roll around in the dark go
and troll and bark with the rest of the mutts who slut it
up after dusk ya pencil-dicked-half-slit-pocket-broke-
beer-bellied-cock-eyed-limp-wristed-ass-swishin-day-
drinkin-un-thinking-lilly-livered-fish-smelling-*faggots.*

Information on this playwright may be found at:
www.smithandkraus.com.
Click on the AUTHORS tab.

Dramatic

Tano, twenties to thirties, Hispanic. A drag queen.

TANO: Ok, hi, I'm Tano Rodrigez Santana "Hope" de la Cruz of one-hundred-and-tenth-street, 6 foot, switch-hitter, Gemini, hi . . . Whatever *you* are? You got guts. Walking around in the daylight, looking like *that,* looking like— (—my God, girl, *go with it—)* So you're quick. Quicker than me. Congratulations. But that's it. That's *it.* Mika and me? When we go out? We're looking to *ball,* we don't buy drinks. I get them, and he gets them, but you don't; So you have to be Bitchy. Cause that's all you have. That's why you gotta dress like that, look like that, *como la puerca de Juan Bobo. Next time* you tuck your dick in between your legs *leave some room to walk,* bow-legged *bitch,* tricky black witch, grab a spike dust if off and sit—And while you're at it!—fuck off! Cause if you expect us to carry you around like a float then you're gonna wind up carried out DEAD like that drunk tub of guts Judy Garland.

Information on this playwright may be found at:
www.smithandkraus.com.
Click on the AUTHORS tab.

Seriocomic
Davis, forties to fifties, white

Davis is an executive for a sneaker company. He asks Thomas, a designer who is black, about a new sneaker. He wants to know if black kids will buy it—because if black kids buy it, white kids will too.

DAVIS: Oh. I see. I'm the white guy right now. Is that it? Hm? I can see that look you're giving me. It's okay. You're right. I'm just a salesman. The 16's were your design. Your brilliance. Personally, I found them silly looking but we've got kids killing each other in the streets for those things. Now, white kids see that and they respect it. It's stupid, I agree, but they do. They're taking notice and we did that. How? By selling the ghetto! Black kid shoots someone for a pair of our shoes, white kid says "now that's something *real!* Something *authentic!*" They want it because they don't understand it. It's beyond the purview of their bullshit sheltered lives of video games and Twitter-Face. We *need* our brand to accepted by real black America so we can become *real* to the posers of *white* America! You wanna know how we beat Nike? Hm? When it's white kids killing for our shoes. Then we win. Who knows why people do these things. It's ghetto shit. I'm from Chicago and I still don't understand it. The point is, *perception*. Kid gets shot, in the ghetto, his shoes are missing—happens to be *our* shoes.

Dramatic
Peter, twenties, white

*After weeks of apologizing for being white, Peter finally
tells his therapist, a black woman, that he's sick of feeling
guilty.*

PETER: What more do I have to do?! Huh!? I *feel* for your
people! Okay? The struggle? The, the *plight?*! I have
professed my sins! Every week I come to you, contrite!
And out there, all the time, in different ways! I am sorry!
Okay?! I AM SORRY FOR MY PEOPLE! They *suck*!
Whatever they did, whenever they did it, I renounce
them! THEY ARE RENOUNCED! Jesus! I'm tired
of paying for shit I didn't do! Slavery! Oppression! 40
acres and the Jim Crow Laws! I didn't bring you people
over here!

    (beat)

So, I see these black kids on the subway. They look a little
sketchy and I think, "hey, maybe I should go to the other
side of the train'—but no! Because then I say to myself,
'who are *you* to judge?! They're probably very smart
educated kids! Who am I to assume that just because
they're African American, they don't read Sartre?!' But
guess what?! They pulled a *fucking gun* on me anyway!
It didn't matter what I thought! So fuck them! And fuck
guilt!! I'm tired of it!! Watching my tongue, policing
every syllable that comes out of my mouth! So, do me
a favor, will you? Tell every black person or African
American that you know that it wasn't me! Can you do
that? Vouch for me?! Huh? IT! WASN'T! ME!

    (beat)

Whoa. That felt really good. Was that a *breakthrough?* Is
that what they call it or whatever? I'm sorry if I scared

you—did I? Jesus, that was amazing! Well . . . I guess I should probably go. Thank you.

Seriocomic
Davis, forty to fifty, White

Davis is talking to Thomas, a black shoe designer for the company he used to run. Davis has just lost his job because of his "insensitivity" toward African Americans in the work place. And now he has nothing.

DAVIS: I did everything they asked. Tried to be more sensitive, say the right things, I really did—you can ask Frederick Douglas! He says I'm using the black man. Fine. So I killed the 16 ad. And they killed me. So, 'sup now, nigga!?

(off his look)

Oh. What? You don't like me using your precious N word? Hm? Did I steal from you? The one thing you have that's yours? A word? Yeah, well, Sky Shoes used to be yours too, didn't it? A black shoe for black people. Well, we stole that too. Welcome to America! Welcome to creamy whiteness!

(beat)

But now that we're on the subject of mine and yours, let's think about this: what do you own, Thomas? Hm? What does the black man have when all the dust has settled? Your history? Your so called culture? Wrong! Bought and sold years ago—just like ours. Watered down. Processed and paid for. Your identity's been whittled down to nothing more than a movie, a TV show, rap song, a commercial about a fucking basketball shoe. You are a cliché borrowed from clichés that we created! So, reach for the sky, bitches! But, hey, no, you have your pain, right? Your daily struggles? A black man in a hard white world? Bullshit! No one owns their pain! The second you use it for currency, it's lost forever. Trust me. And we'll sell it out the second someone's offering something better. So, don't rely on your pain for your power. Your guilt is nothing more than an advertisement for a product you don't own anymore. Sorry, Thomas, but we're all part of the same infomercial. Looking for the one thing that's not for sale.

Dramatic
Carmine, late thirties

Carmine has pinned Chad to the kitchen floor and is assert-
ing his position as the undisputable head of the household.
He has taken Chad's place—indeed, his identity—and
will not relinquish anything. Through this entire speech,
Carmine restrains Chad on the floor.

CARMINE: She's just protecting her territory. See, that's
how survival goes in the wild. Here's a valuable lesson:
First thing a wild animal does when it's threatened is
distract the other animal with whatever it responds to
most, which, with you, seems to be words, right—See?
It attacks when it's got the right amount of attention, see
how easy that was? Now let's you and me set some terms.
She says you're her uncle. You say you're her brother. I
say I don't know you from Adam. So, then how *do* we
know you're who she says you are, or who *you* say you
are, or none of the above? Intuition. What? Intuition.
What? INTUITION! *Intuition?!* Gah gah gah ... *Whose?*
Mine. WHY? 'Cause I'm on fucking *top.* And you know
what my intuition says? First, it says: "Chad — " It says
"Chad, you worked for this. Hours and days and months
... stop with the thrashing, good boy ... years busting
your ass building other people's homes, building other
people's peace and quiet and peace of mind, you deserve
some peace, some quiet, and some peace of mind, too.
Some safety from the shit of this world, from the thieves
and killers and the gangs of raccoons and whatever the
hell else smells bad and lurks around outside that door.
And you finally had it, and then you threw it all away, you
fucked it all up, faster than you could say "Thank you,
dear lord, for my tiny piece of this awful fucking action."

My intuition says: "So, what are you gonna do now that you've got it again? You gonna throw it away like the first time, or you gonna make sure it stays yours?" NOPE, no moving, just listening now. My intuition says: "And so who is *this* guy? What's *he* done for you? He gave away something he didn't want. No, worse: something couldn't ever've been his in the first place! What's he done *since* then? He's stolen from you. He's damaged your property. And now he's trying to damage the delicate infrastructure of your household." Easy, breathe normal, there, exactly. I like my new sister, or . . . whoever she is. I like my new dad, or whoever *he* is. And I like Chad, the Chad I know, the one's been living here as long as I have. Whoever *he* is. I care about these people. You? What do you bring to the table? You may be who you say, but I don't think I know you. So my intuition says "Chad, you would be absolutely justified in taking this piece of trash so far out of your house—the house you worked so hard for—and making sure it is completely and totally impossible for him to ever find his way back here again." Tell you what, though, I do have a heart. So here's the deal. You want to survive this moment better than most? Let's give it a shot, see if you can fit in. You remember what you'd cry out as a kid when someone was doing this to you? You remember?

Seriocomic
Bowen, seventies to eighties

Bowen is practicing what he wants to tell his lover by rehearsing the speech in front of an unstable male hustler he's just invited into his home for a cherry limeade.

BOWEN: *Flores! Flores para los pendejos!* The most godawful production of *Streetcar Named Desire* I've ever seen! I doubt you're rushing off to buy tickets, but I won't allow you to even consider it.

(*Drinks.*)

The director had an inspired idea: a black Blanche. He even renamed the character: Noir Dubois. A long program note about casting against type. Directors who write program notes should write their own goddamn plays.

(*Drinks.*)

I'm sorry, terribly sorry—that's not at all what I wanted to talk about. I mostly just want to apologize. Don't interrupt, please, or it'll never come out. At the end of one's life, one thinks about tidying things up. We live a rather tidy life as it is, except for a few dangling threads, some un-catalogued remnants. I won't say I feel guilty for abducting you from Arizona, but I do realize what you've given up. I took you away from the Taliesen community, a brotherhood, practically a cult, and initiated you into another. You loved modern design, clean lines, and I brought you—rococo. Complicated, overdone, messy. Ancient houses covered in vines, warped, teetering drunkenly on the verge of collapse, and you're the savior. You sneak in an I-beam here, pour a foundation there, the old plantation is propped up ready for the tourists, and the kudzu never even rustled.

(Drinks.)

I am . . . immensely grateful. Have I ever said so? Immensely. I'm partial to beauty, and beauty's what you do, what you *are*. It's my weakness—and don't say "one of many" because all my other flaws stem from this one—I sacrifice everything for beauty. Our family, our dynasty, is our most beautiful creation, well, not our creation, but ours to preserve, to conserve, to renovate. I am aware of your sacrifice. I am aware of your beauty. Why else do you suppose I call you Lady Hideous? What else can I do in the face of such beauty?

Information on this playwright may be found at:
www.smithandkraus.com.
Click on the AUTHORS tab.

House Of The Rising Son
Tom Jacobson

Dramatic
Trent, thirties to forties

Trent is presenting a formal talk on parasites at a confer-
ence at Tulane, and breaks down because his lover has
just been murdered by a hustler.

TRENT: One of the most important life principles—if you're
a parasite—is that of optimal virulence. Just how much
can you take from the host—how much food, how much
blood—before you kill it? Killing the host often means
the parasite dies as well. If tapeworms ate all our food,
if hookworms sucked all our blood, we'd die and so
would they. Self-regulation is important for all species,
not just parasites. There is, however, one species notable
for its lack of self-regulation: *homo sapiens*. We're close
to fishing out the oceans, polluting all potable water,
and destroying the forests and plankton that provide the
very air we breathe. The earth is our host, and we are its
parasite—a parasite that has far exceeded optimal virulence. Nature tries to fight back. Lurking unknown in the
African jungle until forty years ago, AIDS has killed or
afflicted more than 58 million worldwide. Overcrowded
parts of the world have always been vulnerable to epi-
demics like cholera, yellow fever and the Black Death.
I'm sure Mother Nature has worse viruses up her sleeve,
ready to regulate her most destructive children. Social
ills also increase in overcrowded conditions—suicide,
infanticide, child abuse, and patricide—
    (Pauses for a moment to take a deep breath.)
—All terribly—unfortunate—but remarkably effective
means of reducing the surplus population. Violence
is in our blood—the omnivorous diet that fueled our

remarkable brain size also programmed us to kill—and when there are too many of us, we—kill ourselves. But evolution is smarter than we are, and has provided us with some less horrific forms of regulation. In my last lecture I mentioned that the incidence of homosexuality rises as populations become overcrowded. Homosexuals are—*we* are—an evolutionary advantage to our species, a non-violent alternative to—to—

(Pause)

I'm sorry. I'm—uh—I'm going to have to cut this short. You see, my fa—my, my *lover*, Garrett Varro, was murdered three days ago, so the topic hits a little close to home, and—

(Takes a moment to compose himself.)

Evolution of species takes place imperceptibly over eons. But social evolution can happen in a relative blink of an eye. Homosexuality only got a name a hundred years ago. It only became a movement between fifty and sixty years ago with the Mattachine Society. It only came out of the closet forty years ago with the Stonewall riots. It only garnered national sympathy almost thirty years ago with the advent of AIDS. What did your father think of homosexuality? Your father's father? Society is slowly figuring it out—our counter-evolutionary and anti-reproductive trait keeps popping up in our genes for a reason. We are not an accident, a fluke—we help the species survive. Today's lecture was supposed to be about parasites. It seems I've gotten off track. Perhaps not. Perhaps all of us—all human beings—are truly parasites.

(singing to the tune of "People")

And parasites, parasites who need parasites
Are the luckiest parasites in the world!

Information on this playwright may be found at:
www.smithandkraus.com.
Click on the AUTHORS tab.

Comic
Ethan, thirties

Ethan is talking to Daphne, trying to woo her, to impress her with his ability to understand himself and his past and how it has made him the man he is today. He is earnest, passionate and self-assured. This is a flirtatious yet confessional moment for him.

ETHAN: If you really want to know, fine, I'll tell you, it's a simple story, amusing, okay, here we go: I wanted to be a doctor, but my mother wanted me to be a waiter. I want to learn about the heart, she wants me to serve artichoke hearts with a garlic aioli dipping sauce. I eventually caved and found the best restaurant in town: I walked in and am like, "I want to be a waiter. *Here.* " And he's like, "You have no experience." And I looked him in the eye and am like, "Okay man, I'll be a busser." And he's like "No." And I'm like "I will be a dishwasher." And he's like "No." And I'm like "okay—I'll be a FREE dishwasher." And he's like . . . "No." I don't tell that to many people . . . It never would have happened without your encouragement, Daphne. Your persistence. Your enthusiasm. Your cool hair. I was at a convention. Before the book, in real life, after I left Zenn-La. There was a presentation by: A Man. He spoke for hours and hours on the subject of life, of love, of How To Get Into Buildings. There was fire, images, music. There was something strangely intriguing about him. There actually was a fire, so I never heard the end of his speech but I *trusted* him. There was a sadness behind his eyes and a fierceness to his cadence, he inspired and endeared. He spoke about the uniform of a Pizza Delivery Guy. About its potential. He spoke, and I listened.

Information on this playwright may be found at:
www.smithandkraus.com.
Click on the AUTHORS tab.

How To Get Into Buildings
Trish Harnetiaux

Comic
Roger, twenties

This is Roger's Big Moment. He is finally presenting his presentation at Comic Con this year—it's his guide to survival for the modern man or woman. He believes deeply in his well developed philosophies and has been waiting for this moment, the platform where he will share his ideas with the world . . .

ROGER: Good afternoon Ladies and Gentlemen, Super Heroes and Lords of the Underworld . . . What people, today, in our society, on Earth, don't realize is, that most buildings are just that: *Buildings.* They are buildings with *people* in them. You, or One, may for instance, just walk in the door. Just go into a building and say: "Hey is the superintendent around?" And they're like, "What?" And you say, more forcefully, "Hey—is the super here." And sometimes they say, "No, come back after lunch." And you should just say "cool" or something and just hang out for a bit, outside or at Starbucks and then, go back after lunch and start it all again. *Persistence.* You may think you know what you want to "study" or "be" but I'm telling you right now, don't go running around like a child saying "I'm going to be a Doctor when I grown up." Because you'll be lucky if you're a Waiter. *Lucky. So, stop speculating everyone*! You know? Right now you're all just *speculating. Speculating.* The great thing that I was never told and that I wish I knew at a much younger age is this: The world is just a bunch of people dude. You have to be ready to BE one of them. And you can be annoying or persistent—that's totally fine! One way modern men, and women, meet people is to dress as a common Pizza Delivery Guy, or Gal, and enter a building. Tips to ensure entrance include: Make sure you carry the pizza box as if there is a pizza inside. People apparently will let someone with a Pizza in ANYWHERE. "I'm here to see Mr. Carmichael on the 21st floor." "Go right up." "Nancy from accounting ordered a deep dish Hawaiian, which floor is she on again?" "11. Lucky Nancy!" Whether there's a pizza actually IN the box or not, that's up to you. BECAUSE YOU ARE JUST A DUDE TRYING TO FIGURE OUT A WAY INTO A BUILDING. Into a club. It's one big club, and with persistence, if you stop speculating, and if you show up ready to deliver a pizza, you'll have a fair chance of getting in. So, be sure you show up with a pizza box and get ready for a waterfall effect or snowball effect of life's big elements to start happening to you. They'll be like:

Grab a chair!

There's your desk!

Here's your cool new cards!

That's your phone!

Meet your wife!

There's your kids!

Board meeting at noon!

Last one to the diner has to buy! *Now look at you.* You're in the building, in the club, hell you're on your way to being President of the club. I for one, couldn't be more proud because it's an awful world out there, but look at you, you just made it. You made it.

Information on this playwright may be found at:
www.smithandkraus.com.
Click on the AUTHORS tab.

Hurricane
Nilo Cruz

Dramatic
Aparicio, twelve, Caribbean

Aparicio, feeling guilty that his father has suffered an accident because of his misbehavior, is praying to God.

APARICIO: My poor mother. My poor father. It's because of me he is like this. It's because of me this happened to him. I can't stop thinking about it. Last night I could hardly sleep, and when I managed to close my eyes I dreamed of him. He was being swept up in the air by a roaring wind, and he was screaming for his life as he fell into the sea. Then he tried to hold on to a rock, but the sea kept pulling him down to the bottom. And he had to swim for his life, while the big waves were pounding hard against him to drown him. It was so terrible. He couldn't come up to the surface to breathe. —This morning I thought of going to church to confess my sins, but the priest must be busy. The church is full of so many people who've lost their homes that he wouldn't have time to listen to me. And the priest wouldn't do anything except make me repeat ten Ave Marias, which is stupid because then the Virgin would think I'm stuck in one prayer like a broken record. Then I thought of going to the police station and turning myself in for committing this crime, which I really didn't commit, but I feel guilty like a criminal, and I find it hard to live with myself now that my father is like this. And my mother . . . my poor mother, I feel so bad for her, too. My mother who's afraid that my father has forgotten who she is and he won't see her with the same eyes he used to.

Information on this playwright may be found at:
www.smithandkraus.com.
Click on the AUTHORS tab.

HURRICANE
Nilo Cruz

Dramatic
Forrest, late forties to early fifties

Forrest suffers from amnesia and is in a state of confusion. His wife and adopted son have just visited him in the hospital but he has no memory of who they are in his life.

FORREST: Who is this woman, and who is this boy who are claiming to be my wife and son? How come I don't know who they are? She's kind, this wife I'm supposed to be married to, and so is the boy. But I feel nothing in common with them. I've been asked to write what I know, what I don't know, what I see, what I feel, what I think, what I dream . . . I gather someone will read what I write: a lady in an office who studies memories, a man who studies dreams, handwriting, the memory of words. Maybe no one will pay attention to what I have to say. Or maybe someone will ponder at length my writing, my dreams and deduce some meaning, some logic, since they've also asked me to record my dreams. All I know, this is my third day writing. I guess I'm bound to reveal or say something they want to hear. It could be today, tomorrow or maybe never.

   (with frustration)
I just don't know what that is! I only know the days have become formless, shapeless, nebulous . . . crowds of people, dirt, dilapidation, destruction, fragments, panic, desperation, dispersion . . . dead trees obstruct the road when I step outside. Why are there so many people with bundles? Why are they praying? Why are they cursing? Last night I had a dream . . . a dream of a young girl crossing the railroad tracks by a train station. And it wasn't just

a dream. I recognized the place. I'd been there before. I know that place where the girl was. Who is she?! Who is she?! Who is she?! Who are you???!!!

Information on this playwright may be found at:
www.smithandkraus.com.
Click on the AUTHORS tab.

Dramatic
Aparicio, twelve, Caribbean

*Aparicio, feeling helpless and guilty for his father's illness,
looks at his reflection in a puddle of water and speaks to
it.*

APARICIO: All I wanted to do today is run to you, my very
own puddle made by the rain, where the tadpoles swim
freely. Where it is so peaceful and private, because I can
look at my reflection in the water and see the tadpoles
swimming happily all over my face. And it makes me feel
good and happy, because when they swim in my reflection I start to forget things, like everything that happened
to my father. Because the truth is that what happened
to him, should've happened to me. I am the son of the
hurricane not him. The tadpoles understand all of this.
They always understand my thoughts and all of what I
am. Last week the doctor did some kind of procedure on
me. He drew liquid out of my lungs, because they were
filling up with water. A sign . . . a sign that the goddess
in the depths of the sea wants me to go to her. Today I
think my lungs are filling up again, because I feel short
of breath. Sometimes I hang upside down from a tree
to see if the water will come out. Or I go for a swim. I
figure that if all waters meet, the waves hidden inside my
body would want to meet the sea. And, now and then, I
have the sensation of breathing under water. A strange
sensation that is! Something I can't quite understand.
There are days I wonder what color the water inside me
is, and if fish could actually live there, and if they could
swim in and out of my mouth. Then I could keep them
in a glass of water and look at them when I feel lonely
and need company.

(He looks up and addresses the gods of the winds and the goddess of the sea.)

Bring my father back. Bring him back . . . bring him back . . . bring him back to his old self. Hear my prayer, god of hurricanes, god of winds . . . Listen to my prayer, Ye-mayá Olokun, goddess of the sea. Bring back the man he used to be. His name is Forrest Hunter. He slept on these sheets and used to wear these shirts. Bring him back. If you bring him back I'll give myself to you.

Information on this playwright may be found at:
www.smithandkraus.com.
Click on the AUTHORS tab.

If You Start A Fire (Be Prepared To Burn)
Kevin Kautzman

Seriocomic
Chris, twenties

Chris, a college dropout with two years of undergraduate philosophy under his secondhand belt, drives a local truck route. He arrives home to the apartment where his cohabitating waitress-girlfriend Lucy busily prepares a presentation, working toward her MBA. She only wants to sell out if they'll just let her. It is revealed Chris has been fired for punching a coworker, and so, with their backs against a financial wall, Chris attempts to convince Lucy they should start a livecam sex website . . . with her as the star.

CHRIS: You can quit waiting tables. We'll work from home. Manage our own schedules. We'll take a holiday whenever we want. And nobody will touch you. You'll serve up an idea of yourself, and you'll get your life back in exchange. You will transcend your body. You'll be like an angel. A sex angel! We can get by on my unemployment while we launch a personal, insider website. It's all about the impression of access. And it has to be hot! That's what we'll call it! Hot . . . heat . . . something . . . America? Hot. Heat. America. America in Heat dot com! It's perfect! Yeah. We take a set of still photos, do a teaser trailer, generate buzz, and sell a subscription for insider content and access to a live webcam and chat room. There are vast networks where people register to access adult content. It is the twenty-first century! People don't live ethically! We can't. We can only live aesthetically! We live in a house of mirrors built on a house of cards built on a foundation of sand! And I'm telling you there is freedom in hopelessness! God or whatever isn't going to descend from heaven and scold you because you show your tits and ass to strangers for money. This machine is powerful. It's a magic box! It can connect us to people with money who want what we have! Youth. And beauty. And purity. Yeah. That's how we'll market you. You're the girl next door. Apple pie. A rainy day at the cabin. You're stranded and without firewood, but someone's at the door with some wood, and he's going to help keep you warm inside your blanket. Which is an American flag! Boom! Think about it. Nobody cares whether we have any dignity. Insurance. What happens if you get pregnant? We'd have to beg. And I don't want to beg. And I don't want to take out any more loans. They only care if you pay them to care. Socialism lost. Everything's for sale. You can build a cult, a umm . . . a fandom. When people subscribe to your website, you make money. Look at it like this: ten thousand people at ten dollars a year is a hundred thousand dollars. With that kind of money we could finally afford to stop renting. Buy a house. Start a family. You can golf!

Information on this playwright may be found at:
www.smithandkraus.com.
Click on the AUTHORS tab.

It Is Done
Alex Goldberg

Dramatic
Jonas, thirties

Jonas is speaking with Ruby, a stranger he has met at a rural bar in the middle of nowhere during a wind storm. He has confessed to Ruby that he is on the run from a terrifying dream that haunts him, but until this moment has refused to describe the dream, which he has kept a secret from everyone in his life. Because of the fatigue of constantly being on the run, and because he is convinced he will never see this stranger again, he agrees to tell her his dream.

JONAS: Oh. Okay. Well. In my dream I'm in my childhood neighborhood. I'm my age, but everything is how I remembered it. I'm walking with my childhood best friend Marty, but he's still 11 or 12. There is this creek . . . in my dream, not in real life . . . there is this creek, and Marty and I go there to build a dam. We bring a shovel to scoop out dirt and we watch the water build up as a lake on one side, and everything is dry out on the other side. So we finish the dam when this kid shows up. I can't remember his name, but he goes to our school. A real bully. Marty and I finish building the dam when this kid came out of nowhere and kicks his way through it. Demolishes it in like ten seconds, with a stupid grin on his face. I'm still holding the shovel, and I guess I go blank. That's what it felt like, going blank. The next thing I know he's on the ground, and he's bleeding so fast. I don't know how blood really flows, but in my dream it almost gushed out of him. It's unbelievable, there was blood everywhere, all over him, his face, and into the stream. And all I hear is the thwack of hitting him, and then him groaning. Over and over. And then the thwack sounds different. And feels different. And he doesn't groan anymore. I throw down the shovel and just look at him. And quickly, Marty picks up the shovel and starts digging a hole. I can't figure out what he's doing, is he panicking and digging for no reason? Then I get it, and I start using my hands and the hole gets bigger, and bigger, and my arms ache, and my neck hurts, and I can feel the dirt pulling away at my fingernails, and then we stop and look at the hole. And then I roll the kid in. His feet, his legs are at an odd angle, they don't fit. So I adjust him. Bend his knees. Move his feet around. His feet still don't fit. His shoes are high tops. Converse. Chuck Taylors. I unlace them and take them off, and his feet fit. Then we bury him. It's much quicker this way. I use the shovel and Marty watches. He's holding the shoes and he's watching me shovel. And then we're done. With that. We build another dam, and the area where we buried the kid is soon a shallow pool. And the blood washes away, and it's done. We stop and look around, and it looks good. And then, clear as day, I hear the dead kid say "that's okay, I'll just get you when you sleep." What really scares me comes next. The dream is over. I wake up, in bed. Drenched in sweat, his words echoing in my ear. I'm breathing hard, and then it all comes back to me and I realize where I am. Maybe moonlight out a window. Maybe the glow of the alarm clock. Maybe a light under the door. Maybe a TV on. Then I calm down. Catch my breath. Start to relax. Everything is okay. And then . . . I feel a hand on my throat, tightening. I don't see it, it's still dark. But I feel it, tightening around my neck, and I feel hot breath on my face, and it's the dead kid, and as he tightens, I hear him whisper "it is done." And I can't breathe. And then I wake up.

Seriocomic
Gopal, teens

Gopal has just met this dude named Jesus, who has ridden to India on a camel from some place called Galilee. He's a wannabe punk rock musician who would rather be anything than a mung bean farmer.

GOPAL: My father is a mung bean farmer. Do you know what that means?

(*Silence.*)

Exactly. It means that I'm a mung bean farmer. But somehow, as you can see, I am not that. One day I was farming mung beans at the mung bean farm and I was like man I don't even like mung beans. So I put down my mung bean picker in the middle of the mung bean field, took off my mung bean picking shoes and walked away. There was a time when this was not possible. Our traditional Hindu worldview, as articulated in the *Vedas*, teaches one to strive not for mobility within the rigid social caste system, which was prevalent in the Indos region at the time (for such mobility was impossible), but rather to strive for a mobility of spirit, and a freedom from temporal earthly trappings. Including our material bodies and the mung beans that surround us. Yet as the teachings of the Buddha begin to spread throughout the Indos, certain localities have been able to challenge this established social order in a way that eliminates these socially constructed mandates. Naturally there are residual symptoms of these antediluvian paradigms within the idiosyncratic jurisdictions of disparate and autonomous municipalities, since we have no centralized or prototypical rubric for cross-border or transnational governance. But when we learn that there is no self, then our consciousness becomes aware of our surroundings in a harmonious and peaceful state of connectivity. Our lives are nothingness, which is to say they are void of suffering, and if all is nothing, then nothing is all, and so there is no difference between nothing and everything.

Information on this playwright may be found at:
www.smithandkraus.com.
Click on the AUTHORS tab.

Dramatic

Jesus, late teens

Jesus has come to India from some far off place called Galilee to escape the fate that awaits him back home. He has fallen in love with a slave girl named Mahari, to whom he confesses a secret.

JESUS: I lied. [about] My father, because the day that I left, from Galilee, my father, he . . . he told me something. It was my 18th birthday, we had a party, and at the end we're cleaning up, silent, quiet, like always, but then he He tells me that. That he is not my real father. But was directed by an angel to raise me as his own. That I am the Son of God. That before I was born, God spoke to him, saying that I have a certain destiny, that I will become King of the Jews, bear the weight of the sins of the world, that in my suffering and my death I will bring salvation to all humankind.

(Silence.)

And so I told him to go fuck himself.

(Silence.)

I spent my whole life watching the wrong man. I studied him, tried to *be* him, wondered if I have what it takes to be that. And he's not much of a carpenter. In fact he frankly sucks at it. He's not the best husband, not the best father. He's just a man. And that's awesome. Because I thought it meant I'd never have to be more than that myself. But if he's not my father. Then. Who am I? Right? Who am I?

Comic
Barry, thirties to fifties

Barry, an agent, is trying to sell his client, an actor named Ashraf, on a role in movie which is clearly a mass of anti-Muslim clichés.

BARRY: If you spent two seconds vacationing out of your ass you might discover what's actually around you—and that *maybe*: the director is coming on board to address the very concerns you care about, like justice, fairness, and all that other sissy shit which I respect except when you're being a prima donna about it. The family! Of course it's the family, look at what happens. It's on every page: the over-consumption, the excesses, the mindless gluttony. A family with enough food on their table to feed hundreds. And how that—. I mean look at what it's saying: The way that turns us into a plundering machine that has to bully the world to keep our tables full and our bellies stuffed and how that blows back into our homes in an oh-so-ironic way. The whole film is an indictment of that! The monkey playing the star-spangled banner, for chrissakes. Should there be footnotes for you? . . . The
(Makes quotation marks.)
"bad guys" who burst in are the "provocateurs." They trigger the issues Julius wants to tackle. I'd bet a percentage point he has a little twinkle in his eye for these thugs because they're the ones who help him get into the heart of this film. Through them we get the *wakeup call.* "Change or else." "Stop being the greedy, bloated ugly American or suffer the ax of hubris and die." Think Dr. Strangelove. Think Kubrick. Think anything but what you're thinking because it's *just plain wrong.*

(slight beat)

And even if this film was everything you think it is, you should be fucking grateful you were asked to play a stereotype in a Julius Steele film. He would be on your resume for the rest of your life. Your ingratitude, *that's* what's offensive. I swear to god I'm ready to recommend another actor.

Information on this playwright may be found at:
www.smithandkraus.com.
Click on the AUTHORS tab.

Dramatic
Ken, thirty-seven

Ken, an emotionally unstable writer who is separated from his wife. He has rented a basement apartment from Pete, a blue-collar Good Samaritan. Pete takes Ken under his wing. But the unexpected arrival of Ken's mother sends Ken into a spiral of despair. After a night of drinking and brooding, Ken unburdens himself to Pete.

KEN: My mother—my own *mother*—told the woman I loved—the only woman that I will ever love—that she caught me—molesting a little girl. And even that wasn't enough for her. She told Wendy there was one other girl that she knew about . . . that she *knew* about, for Chrissake! One other girl—and one boy. It was a lie, I swear to God it was a lie. Why did she lie? That's what I kept asking myself. Is she crazy? Has my mother always been crazy? And then it hit me. Like a fucking freight train. Mom couldn't stand seeing me happy with Wendy . . . because she's always wanted me herself. Sick, sick. Maybe she doesn't even know it. But nothing else makes sense. And once I saw that, a thousand other things fell into place. And you wonder why I can't stand to be near that woman? Suppose somebody told a lie about you. Suppose somebody spread a rumor that you had—touched one of the kids on the team. "No, not Pete Vitale! We know Pete, not Pete!" But it would be out there. Once it's out there, once somebody says it, it takes on a life of its own. You hear something like that, you can't make yourself un-hear it. No, Wendy didn't believe it. She was 99 percent sure. But she wanted to not believe it just a little bit more. And one night—we were arguing, we were a little wasted—it came out. That *filth* my mother told her came out. She swore she didn't believe it, all she wanted was to hear it, to hear me say it wasn't true. She was 99 percent sure, but she wanted that extra one percent. And I was stoned and sick to my stomach, and that filth was coming out of *her* mouth, and she shouldn't have needed to ask, she should have had more faith in me, she never should have asked, and it's a terrible thing, you should never raise your hand to a woman, I know that, not ever, but I had to stop the filth and the lies, and it was the only thing I was guilty of, I swear. It was the only thing I was guilty of. But you don't get to take something like that back, either. And that was a year ago and she's been punishing for it ever since.

(in tears)

And Wendy won't come back, and my mother won't go away, and I'm dying. I am fucking drowning here, Pete. I am surrounded by liars and betrayers and there's nobody I can trust. I'm 37 years old and my life is over. I'm a dead man with no dick.

Information on this playwright may be found at:
www.smithandkraus.com.
Click on the AUTHORS tab.

LIGHTNING FROM HEAVEN
Scott Sickles

Dramatic
Alexanochkin, mid-thirties

*Alexanochkin, an interrogator for the Soviet KGB, is trying
to establish that a woman named Olga was the model for
the character of Lara in Boris Pastnernak's subversive,
anti-Soviet, novel Doctor Zhivago.*

XANOCHKIN: Hm. Pasternak paints Tonya so lovingly. She
is kind, patient, sweet . . . her only flaw appears to be her
justifiable fits of jealousy over her husband's wayward
affections. And Lara . . . Pasternak endows her with only
the most sordid elements of Zinaida Nikolayevna's past,
absolving his wife of her sins, at least in fiction, by passing
them on . . . to you. And who are you—or rather, who is
Lara? The adulteress he keeps hidden away. Interpretation.
Subjectivity. Parallels. It's those sorts of things that get
you creative types in trouble . . . in art and in life. Let's
eliminate any room for misinterpretation. I will ask you
a question. It is a question I have asked you before and
often. All you have to do is say "yes" or "no." Between
the two, there is no wrong answer. Once all this is done,
you will be released. You will go home to your daughter.
To your life. Today. With one utterance . . . one breath
. . . I guarantee your freedom.
    (Pause)
Are you Lara?

*Information on this playwright may be found at:
www.smithandkraus.com.
Click on the AUTHORS tab.*

Lawrence Harbison   103

Dramatic
Tom, twenties

Tom Powers, a Hollywood movie star, explains to his agent, Jane, why, against her better judgment, he must participate in a live televised debate on a prime time political talk show.

TOM: You know something, Jane? You are absolutely right. It is entirely about ego. And that's because most of the time guys like me are perceived as being spoiled, out of touch, and irresponsible jackasses. But I think you and I both know different. That's not who I am. I was born and raised on two hundred acres of the most beautiful farmland in Iowa, and my father and mother made damn sure that they instilled in me a sense of honor, duty, and integrity. But I been working this town going on three years now, and don't get me wrong, I love what I do, I love my job, and when I'm working I give it one hundred and ten percent. But I am more than just a pretty face on a one-sheet. I am intelligent, and I am articulate. I speak three languages, four, if we count English. And I went to a school which taught me that Art is more than just posing for the cover of Vanity Fair. I was taught that Art, in its best and brightest form, should be an expression of the human will, and of the human psyche, and that it should reflect reality. But you know what's the onion? That in the grand scheme of things what does Art really matter, hm? Does it erase poverty? Feed the hungry? Clothe the naked? Create infrastructure? Ease the pain and suffering of those who are in pain and suffering? No. It doesn't. Not directly anyway. But you know what Art can do, though? It can get people thinking. I can use my celebrity to help influence the debate instead of sitting comfortably on the sidelines like some sort of lame, chicken-ass wannabe whose only concern is how can I build a bigger house in Malibu beach.

Dramatic
Tom, twenties

In the middle of a live televised debate on a prime time political talk show, Tom, a Hollywood movie star, finds a way to successfully argue in defense of the second amendment to the U.S. Constitution.

TOM: Just out of curiosity how many people do you think there are in this country that own guns that want the government to come in and take them away? Let me tell you something, Madeline, and it has nothing to do with personal freedom or public safety. Just you tell me, what happens when you start striking down stuff that's already on the books? What happens next, hm? We're talking, here, about one of the freedoms we have taken for granted in this country since its inception. We strike it down what's it going to take to strike down another, huh? And one that you could argue that the founding fathers didn't take the time to set down themselves? That it's something post hoc, after the fact, like, say, numbers thirteen and nineteen, which would be the abolition of slavery and women's suffrage respectively. If we do that, if we make that argument, then what kind of precedent does that set? And is that the first step in auctioning off the Bill of Rights, and if so how easy would we have just made it for the next guy to do exactly that?

Dramatic
Tom, twenties

Tom, a Hollywood movie star, must defend himself after being backed into a corner by his opponent during the height of a live televised debate on a prime time political talk show.

TOM: You wanna know why the right feels the way it does, Madeline? Because all we want is to be left alone. And then people like you come along with your eastern academic mother-knows-best attitude to teach us all a lesson we so richly deserve whether we asked for it or not. So, let me just say this, how do you think a person who feels talked down to, ridiculed, and then patronized by someone claiming to be their neighbor will ever hope to feel anything but contempt toward that neighbor? Because you can disagree with me, and the people like me, all you want. You can disagree with our opinions, you can disagree with our lifestyle, you can disagree with the way we raise our kids. But what you do when you relegate anyone that's either religious or raised in a small town somewhere to second class status it only serves to point out the hypocrisy in your own argument. You don't think it's our opinions that are stupid. You think we're stupid and so we have those opinions. That is why we will never be able to have a genuine dialogue of ideas in this country, Congresswoman. Because of people like you.

Dramatic
Jeff, thirty

Jeff's fiancée, Sarah, died of cancer. He tells Lisa, a strange woman with whom he has begun a relationship, about a dream he had which torments him.

JEFF: I had a dream. I woke up in the middle of the night. I was walking along the seashore with Sarah and we were picking up starfish, and watching the strange thing the light does when you step in wet sand. You know? It's sort of like a halo around your foot. Like the water is being pushed away or something. Physics. It's like, totally beautiful. And there are starfish of all different colors lining the beach, and she's in her wedding dress and I'm in the tux and I bend down to pick up this like ridiculously bright green starfish or something and I look up and I see her and then she becomes you. And you are her and she is you and you're smiling and I'm confused but we keep picking up these blue and red and purple starfish and walking along this beach, and there's a red and white lighthouse in the distance and this kind of storm cloud brewing behind it, out over the water. And we're holding hands and I feel this wetness in my palm, and I look at you and there's a stream of blood running down your arm. It's coming out of your ears now and and and you start to wobble, and you drop the starfish, and you're like standing on the sand with this rainbow of these hundreds of like miniature multi-colored iridescent starfish twinkling around you and you die . . . Like all the blood drains out of your body and your dress is turning red, and you float out on this raft of totally unrealistic looking perfectly shaped cartoon-like starfish, out into the ocean, out into the cylindrical dark grey storm cloud. And then I woke up . . . I had that dream and I didn't think that I could ever call you or see you again.

Information on this playwright may be found at:
www.smithandkraus.com.
Click on the AUTHORS tab.

MANNING UP
Sean Christopher Lewis

Comic
Raymond, thirty-five

Raymond is talking to his best friend Donnie in his Long Island Man Cave. The two men are terrified of the fact they are both about to become fathers and in this monologue Raymond describes his innate want to protect his wife from bullies she works with and his complete failure to do so.

RAYMOND: Yeah. I mean she works harder than anyone I know. But of our friends and the like . . . she just, I see it. I see how important the place is to her. She's the goddam office manager and this guy J blames her for everything. And you know there's nothing I can do. I'm just power-less. And I keep thinking there's gotta be something I can do. Like I want to beat him up. So the shelter is in this old church, right. Like 1800's or something—I mean the building's falling apart—and it's Sally's job to keep things running. So, she calls me one day in tears. And I've had it, like with this guy, I'm gonna look his address up and I'm going to tear him a new one . . . and Sally says have you looked outside? And I say yeah. And she says it's raining. And she just breaks down. And I'm like what's going on? And she says it's raining in the meeting room. The roof has a break in it . . .

(Demonstrates with hands.)
. . . like this big and water's just pouring in. And they already had the roofers in once and she just keeps crying because she knows this guy is going to blame her . . . So I got in my car and drove over there and I don't know what I'm doing. I bought a bunch of caulk and it was like the *A Team*. She met me at the door and I had these caulk guns and this caulk and I think it was for glass but

whatever—she says "you made it." And it's like an old Bogart movie. She's got that look in her eyes, you know 'help me.' I mean usually it's me that has that look. But I love it . . . And I say, "yeah I'm gonna take care of this. Don't you worry. I'm gonna take care of it good." So I get up there and it's a mess. Water's coming down the roof, it's not getting drained, I'm so drenched my clothes weigh as much as I do. And I start to caulk everything. I'm caulking walls, the ceiling, inside the ceiling, it's just everywhere, I'm using electrical tape to hold it all in. And she's watching me and some of the families are coming in looking. Luckily it's no one else. I DON'T KNOW WHAT THE HELL I'M DOING, MAN. I'm a complete fraud basically. All I know is that ceiling right now has about 40 pounds of caulk in it. And I signed the inside of it "Jeremy"—her boss—"can suck it, signed Sally Guinnesses' husband."

A Measure Of Cruelty
Joe Calarco

Comic
Derek, teens

After committing a heinous bullying crime Derek, a troubled teen, has been sheltered by a bar owner who is wrestling with demons of his own. Derek feels safe and feels he can confide in the older man.

DEREK: I couldn't even get a dog. When I was eight I wanted a dog, you know a man's best friend kinda situation, but he was like, "No way. I'm not picking up after some stanky ass dog. I gotta do enough of that with you." And he was like, "And I don't care how much you promise me you'll do it yourself. You never do anything you say you're gonna do, and I'm not having dog shit stinking up my house 'cause my son's a lazy bum." I got all upset, and I guess that must've made him all marshmallowy inside for a split second 'cause he was all, "Stop crying like a little girl. Shut up, and I'll buy you a hamster" which was like the first and last time he ever gave me anything. And he was all, "Keep it in your room 'cause when you forget to clean up after it, you're the one who'll have to deal with the stanky ass cage." So he mini-vanned my ass over to the pet store and I said to the clerkage all standing around, I said, "I got a name picked out: Bruno. Go get me Bruno the hamster." And they brought me out the most Bruno looking hamster you ever seen. We took him home and like a week later, whack, whack, whack, Bruno pops out some babies. And I was like, "Why'd they tell me it was a boy when it was really a girl?" That was like the first "the world sucks" kinda lie that ever happened to me. But I thought, "Okay, maybe one of them babies can be my Bruno the Second." And I was hanging over the cage peaking in, trying to get a look at which one I was gonna pick, and I noticed this tiny little one, like the mayor of mini-McHamsterville. And it was laying on its side all gasping for breath and stuff. And then his Mama? Dude, she started eating him. I'm not bullshitting you. I tried to stop it. I was screaming and shaking the cage, but the more I did, the faster she ate. And my Dad came in bitching at me to shut up, and then he saw what I was screaming about, and he smiled and said, "Don't worry. That's just her mothering instinct or whatever kicking in." He told me that if one of her babies is too weak she'll eat it knowing it won't survive this world, so it's like her saving her baby from a shitty life. He was all, "Gotta be strong or you'll get eaten alive. That's what she's teaching her other pups. What she's doing right there? That's for them. That's what love is." Douchebag thing to say, right?

Information on this playwright may be found at:
www.smithandkraus.com.
Click on the AUTHORS tab.

Seriocomic
Derek, teens

After committing a heinous bullying crime Derek, a troubled teen, has been sheltered by a bar owner with demons of his own. Derek confides in the older man. While munching on a strawberry pop tart.

DEREK: I'm not bullshitting you. It was just like in that movie with all those Nazis burned up trying to steal all of God's power. Even with just that sliver of a window back there I could see it and I was thinking, "What if it stayed like this?" Like wake up to sizzle, sizzle, bang, bang, flash. Havin' to pull shades at night for even a chance a shuteye. Storing up on Tylenol PM. Get you all dopey. You start slipping into some just before dreamtime state and flash, flash, flash! Flying out of bed wondering where all the paparazzi came from. Stumble to the bathroom and suck down some Nyquil. Fall face first back into your mattress and pow, pow, pow! All those flashes again. But you're so whacked out on over the counter type sleeping aids that all you can do is roll over and reach for some eye lubrication type action making sure all the red's out, making yourself all pretty. Hell, everybody's doing it. We're talking major Visine shortage. Whole cities full of people draggin' ass out onto the front lawns to watch the light show—forgettin' to feed the kids, lettin' the house go to hell. Screw the sofa. Let Fido go to town. Dogs chompin' down on cushion stuffing, shit stains on the shiny new shag. I'm tellin' you everyone's just gonna be loungin' in a lawn chair, twenty four hours, three hundred sixty five days starin' up, up, up at the flash, flash boom. Nobody carin' about nothin' no more. Fruit rotting in the grocery stores. Super markets stinkin' a sour milk.

Nobody buying nothin'. Who needs lean cuisine? Just lean right over, grab a hunk a grass from the green, green, lawn, munchin' down on weedage, snackin' on some snails, starin' up, up, up, smiling. Everybody thinking God sent down some kind of host of angels to snap a family portrait, you know? I am like totally addicted to this strawberry poptartification.

Information on this playwright may be found at:
www.smithandkraus.com.
Click on the AUTHORS tab.

Seriocomic
Bryce, late twenties.

Bryce tries to convince his roommate Sam about the fallacy of true love.

BRYCE: When I was in high school me and my best friend Tyler both had this huge thing for Amy Killingsworth. Total babe and didn't know it. We spent all summer with her waiting for her to like give us a sign or whatever. Anyway, she didn't and by August I was starting to wear my hand down to the bone so I just fucking asked the bitch out. Ended up losing our virginity to each other and fucking like bunnies until school started. And as we were breaking up she tells me in, like, tears that she wished she'd picked Tyler instead, that she'd always liked him better. She said that since I was the one who made the move she just assumed that I must like her more and she wasn't going to turn down a sure thing. Anyway, she and Tyler are, like, divorced now or whatever. But because she's such a flaky bitch I will always have her v-card.

Dramatic
Roger, late thirties

Roger, the head of a Christian Political Action Group,
Roger is fanatical in his convictions He feels all of his
actions are sanctioned by God, and his self-righteousness
is often insufferable.

ROGER: When I was very young, my father had died and
my mother . . . She remarried and this man, my step
father, he came to live in my house, and we never really
got along, he was a very mean person, he resented the
attention I got from my mother I suppose, but I was eight
years old, so I don't know better, I'm a child, but this
man, my stepfather he was very critical of me, and sort of
. . . he found ways to humiliate me, and punish me. And I
could feel my mother turning away from me, I sensed her
love slipping away, and one night in my bedroom I got
down on my knees and prayed for this man to die. I asked
God to punish this man, for him to die a horrible death.
And a few months later my mother came to me and with
tears in her eyes revealed to me that my stepfather was
indeed dying. He had been sick for over a year and they
thought he could beat it, but it was only getting worse,
he only had a short time, and of course I felt terrible. I
had prayed to God and it seemed God had answered my
prayer and now this man was going to suffer. And one
Sunday when my mother was out at church and I had
stayed home to care for my stepfather, I heard a terrible
crash and I ran downstairs and I found my stepfather on
the floor of the bathroom covered in his own excrement,
crawling towards the toilet. And my stepfather looked
up at me and . . . he was the child now, a helpless child,

confused and degraded, by a body that had failed him, and I picked him up and cleaned him off, I wiped the feces from his legs and his . . . I washed him and dragged him back to his bed. And when my mother came home from church, I didn't say anything but merely sat in my room. And in a week or so, he died. God had in a way answered my prayers. A selfish prayer of a selfish child. That incident taught me a powerful lesson. I have never wished for someone to suffer since then, Julie. Even in moments where I feel terrible frustration. In those moments I ask for patience. And forgiveness.

MISTER HART AND MISTER BROWN
Bruce Graham

Comic
Local Historian, old

The Local Historian is speaking to a man who is doing research on a man named Richard Hart, who fought boot-leggers during Prohibition dressed as if he were a hero in a western movie.

LOCAL HISTORIAN: The 50's, that's when it all started to go to hell. Fifty-one, fifty-two—around there. Never forget. Went to see *High Noon*. Gary Cooper playin' a sheriff. Doesn't get any bettern' that. So the movie starts and . . . it was like somebody hit me with a brick. On the screen . . . there's Gary Cooper—Gary Cooper!—and he's actin' like, uhhh . . . like an I-don't-know-what. He's cryin'! The bad guys are comin' and he's bawlin'. He's scared! I mean, what is this—a foreign film or somethin'? Grace Kelly ends up shootin' the bad guy for God's sake. And she's supposed to be a Quaker. I mean, that's wrong on a couple different levels. I couldn't believe it. Gary Cooper doesn't cry. He doesn't beg the townsfolk for help. He straps on his guns, marches down the middle of the street—blam, blam, blam—rides off into the sunset. "Realism." "Psychological westerns." No thank you. You ask me that's when things started to go to hell in this country. Maybe I'm just gettin' old—I don't know. Korea. This Viet Nam mess we're in now . . . I'll be honest with you—I don't know which side I'm supposed to be rootin' for. I'm serious. I watch the news. I read the papers and . . . I got no idea who the good guys are. I gotta' buck says they never make any sorta' Viet Nam movies. Too confusin'. So I don't blame you kids for protestin'—not one bit. We're goin' to hell in a handbasket.

(leaning forward)

I mean, at least westerns used to be a sure thing. Nothin' complicated. Good guys and bad guys. Nice and simple.

(He thinks a moment.)

Let me tell you something: if John Wayne ever starts cryin' I am movin' to Canada.

Seriocomic
Peter, forties to fifties

Peter is a very successful director and producer of low-budget, high-yield porn films. He is speaking to Robert, who knows nothing about the porn business but has seen a scene being shot and is appalled.

PETER: Well, of course, the glamour isn't really there on the set. But once you see the finished product . . . It's kind of like what they say about sausage. Lots of people love to eat it, but it's a business my friend. Like any other business. Except this business is a 35 billion dollar business. That's bigger than the NFL. Look out the window. See those Mc-Mansions on the other side of the ravine? That's the town that porn built, dude. Every house you gaze upon, every car you see, every pool that's shimmering in someone's back yard was paid for by porn. Everybody you see in the Safeway is in the business. Their kids fill the schools and before you know it, *they'll* be in the business. There are 40 million consumers of porn in this great country. It's not about dirty old men wearing raincoats in dark, sticky, decrepit theaters, ya know. That's ancient history. It's Main Street America today. It started with the VCR and really picked up steam with DVDs. But the Internet! The Internet was the mother lode, dude. Shit, today, everybody on the planet watches porn and half of 'em have made some themselves. Housewives, secretaries, CFOs, Boy Scout leaders, men of the cloth, members of the PTA. Little old ladies. Porn is as American as apple pie.
   (Pause, as PETER reflects on the beauty of it all.)
And I own a nice chunk of that empire. I could buy and sell you and your little funeral home a hundred times

over. I drive a fucking Bentley. Know what I paid for that Bentley? Ginny, that piece of ass you're too puritanical to admit you want to fuck? I found that bitch doing the C-list strip club circuit in St. Louis when she was twenty. I classed her up, fixed her teeth, invested in a boob job, changed her name to Osprey Hepburn and made her a star. And look at her today. *Adult Video News* called her the Meryl Streep of group sex. She may not be much of an actress, but if you've ever seen her take on six guys at once—well, if that ain't talent, it oughta be. Who the fuck are you to judge what's dehumanizing? You think people are satisfied with run-of-the-mill porn these days? You gotta constantly come up with shit that's gonna stand out from the crowd. Repulse and attract simultaneously. The secret of my success can be summed up in a single lesson I learned years ago: What shocked people yesterday is predictable today and boring tomorrow. Nobody wants to see that billing and cooing shit. It's played out. Intimacy in porn is like showing a silver cross to a vampire. It's a buzz kill. People don't want tenderness; they want strangers going at each other with as much contempt as they can muster. They want anonymous, insensate, angry people ripping whatever the hell they want out of each other's asses. There's a need in the marketplace for ever more outrageous shit. And nobody fulfills that need like Priapic Productions. We took in sixty million in revenue last year alone. Hey, it's no different from any other business. Same as people like you, who get rich selling cheap metal boxes at five thousand a pop to grieving suckers so they can feel better about partying on while their loved ones rot in the ground. We all gotta make a living. I got a plaque in my office. It says, "If you build it, they will come. But if you wreck it, they will come twice."

Information on this playwright may be found at:
www.smithandkraus.com.
Click on the AUTHORS tab.

THE MONEY SHOT
Adam Cunningham

Dramatic
Muhammad, thirties to forties

During the filming of a low-budget porn film in the Hollywood hills, planes have started dropping out of the sky. Apparently, some sort of nuclear device has exploded in the atmosphere and fried all electronics. Soon, gangs are coming up from the valleys, looting houses and attacking people. Muhammad, a cameraman of Middle-Eastern descent, has made a run for it along with Peter, the director, and Phoebe, a porn actress, who acts under the name "Robin Littlerack." He comes back, alone. He has been shot. The others have asked him what happened to him, and to Peter and Phoebe, aka Robin.

MUHAMMAD: We got to the next house down the hill, but there were people already there. Must have been two dozen of 'em. Tough guys, you know? They were looting the place. We saw . . . we saw a guy—I assume it was the owner—yelling at them to get the hell off of his property. The ring leader walked over and picked up some kind of club—like a tree branch or something. The whole time the guy was yelling at him. Then he just walked up to the guy and hit him on the side of the head with the club. The guy didn't go down at first.Didn't even seem to realize he'd been hit. He kept yelling. Then the guy hit him again. The guy's eyes rolled back in his head and his knees buckled. Then the other guys started beating the shit out of him. We couldn't see what happened once he was on the ground, but we could hear the sound of the beating and the yelling. Then silence. Then there was yelling again and they started to smash windows and trash the house. Fortunately, they didn't see us. We were pretty far up the hill yet and we hid behind a van. We thought they'd see us if we went back up the hill, so we decided to get around them by slipping behind the house across the street and going past them. Well, we followed the driveway to the back, but they had dogs, and the dogs were freaking and so Peter and Robin freaked and started running back toward the road. Their sudden movement really got the dogs going and they chased them. That's when we got separated. So I went down to the next house. I knocked. No answer. Then I saw another group of guys coming. They had a can of gasoline with them. They poured it all over a couple of cars and set fire to them—I have no idea why. It was like a party to them. Insanity. Fucking fools. If that fire spreads . . . I mean, what the fuck kind of response is that to what's happened? Fight chaos with chaos? I didn't dare walk down any farther, so I retraced my steps and ran like hell back here. I saw Peter and Robin sprint out from behind a fence maybe a hundred yards from me. Robin was pretty hysterical. She was screaming. The dogs were chasing her. One of the guys from the group saw what was happening. He pulled out a gun and shot at the dogs. I was afraid he'd hit Phoebe or Peter, but the sound of the first gun shot stopped the dogs in their tracks while Phoebe and Peter ran straight toward the mob. They looked grateful at first, but then the guys started gathering around them. I guess Robin figured out what was going on and she tried to run. Peter, too. They tried to get up an embankment that led to the next house, but the guys caught up with them. I can't say what happened next. I heard Robin scream.

Information on this playwright may be found at:
www.smithandkraus.com.
Click on the AUTHORS tab.

Guillermo Calderón. English translation by Andrea Thome

Dramatic
Aleko, thirty

Aleko, an actor, declares his love for Olga, his company's leading lady whose husband, the playwright Anton Chekhov, has recently died.

ALEKO: Olga, I'm a scab. I didn't have shoes until I was thirteen years old, I drank milk from my mother's and my sister's breasts, and only when they had babies. My father beat me, I never saw him sober and he never looked me in the eye. A priest raised me in his home because he said I knew how to sing and because in the winter I didn't cry from hunger. That's how life was in the country, Olga, and it was beautiful. I wanted to live in the city, but when I got here I saw how some drunks beat a horse to death. I bent down, kissed its eyes and I got stained with blood, Olga. Just like you, stained with blood. That's why when I went to see you at the theater, invited by a woman who paid me to love her, I fell in love with you. Because you are sad, because you appear older than you are, because you know how to walk, because I would like to be like that and dress like that. And since you came to rehearse with us I've had a constant erection. For the last two weeks I've been urinating in the street, my penis freezes, it turns black. I'd love . . . to penetrate you. I love you and I want you to love me, but you won't love me because I'm poor. Don't let my soldier's face mislead you, when I'm naked you'll realize. That's how we poor people are, we have fewer bones and the few that we have are bigger, we're lopsided. I have rat bites on my buttocks. I smell like a woman where I ought to smell like a man and I don't know how to love without wanting to hit, kill, vomit, pray, drink and love some more. The most important organ in my body is my appendix and I want to stick it in your kidney and watch you sweat.

Information on this playwright may be found at:
www.smithandkraus.com.
Click on the AUTHORS tab.

THE NORWEGIANS
C. Denby Swanson

Seriocomic
Tor, thirties to forties

Tor is a Minnesotan of Norwegian descent who, with fellow hit-man Gus, specializes in bumping off ex-boyfriends. In fact, Tor and Gus have been hired by a Texas woman named Olive to kill hers. Their favored murder weapon is a baseball bat.

TOR: Here's what I'm thinking in that moment. The moment of ending a life. It is the single most important moment they will ever have. The end. It's an event they will get to experience only once. Only once. They don't expect it to be happening now. But it is. It is. It is happening now. I want it to go well. Is it possible that a baseball bat isn't the best choice? Might seem that way. Sure. To an outsider. In 1991, the Minnesota Twins won the World Series. It was a magical season. Just magical. We haven't had one like it since. And I was there for the whole thing. The Twins and the Braves were the first two teams in Major League history to start out last and end up first. It's so biblical. Almost prophetic. So restrained. And so—so—so Norwegian. And the last shall be first. So deeply Norwegian. It took the whole seven games. Four at home. We could have been nice and come in second. We could have been true to our nature. But we got up our nerve and we actually won. That's the way that I think about growing the business as well. The Norwegians could be second in market share. Second in revenues. Third, even. And that would be fine. Because inside, we would know ourselves champions, gracious to the competition, we would know it in our hearts. We would even be nice about it. Or we could beat the living crap out of the other team, and win. I

love the Minnesota Twins. I love them with all my heart.
And this is their winning bat.

Information on this playwright may be found at:
www.smithandkraus.com.
Click on the AUTHORS tab.

PALOMA
Anne García-Romero

Dramatic
Ibrahim, late twenties

Ibrahim tells his friend about his father's reaction when he found out Ibrahim is dating a girl who is not a Muslim.

IBRAHIM: I needed some space so I left the hotel, walked around for a while and then decided to take the Metro to *Sol*. I walked out of the station and up the stairs of Big's internet and phone place. I paid five euros for booth six and dialed, knowing my pop would be home, watching some shit on the History Channel. I needed some space so I went out for a walk and decided to call my father. I sat in that booth sweating, my stomach turning, my intestines cramping, my bladder aching, fight or flight, you know? . . . and that fucking phone kept ringing and ringing. [But he picked up] eventually. And I'm like, "Yo, pop." And he's like, *(with slight Moroccan accent)* "What the hell are you doing calling me at one thirty in the morning in Madrid?" And I'm like, "I wanted to chat with you." And then I'm starting to sound like I'm real nervous, you know? At first I was like talking small talk and shit and I knew my pop was getting pissed. *(with slight Moroccan accent)* "What, you run out of money?" And I'm like, "No, pop. I . . . I met someone." And he's like, *(with slight Moroccan accent)* "You get a girl pregnant and I'll kick your ass." And I'm like, "Pop. Her name is Paloma." And he's like, *(with slight Moroccan accent)* "You meet a nice Muslim girl with a Spanish name?" And I'm like, "She's nice. She has a Spanish name. But [she's not Muslim]" And he's like, *(with slight Moroccan accent)* "What about *Sharzad*?" The woman your father had hoped to arrange for you to marry. And I'm like, "Pop. I'm not seeing her anymore." And he's like, *(with slight Moroccan accent)* "Your mother and I know." And then my stomach starts to fuckin' ache and I have to shit real bad and I'm like fuck, I know that tone in his voice. He's like, *(with slight Moroccan accent)* "She called us three days ago. She told us you went to Madrid with your new girlfriend. She told us her name is Paloma. She told us she is Christian." And he proceeded to cuss me out real rapid fire in Arabic, you know. I didn't know shit what he was saying but the energy was serious and I was like double fuck. And then in like his intense English he says things like, *(with slight Moroccan accent)* "You know, God will punish you for your sins and our family's reputation is ruined."

Information on this playwright may be found at:
www.smithandkraus.com.
Click on the AUTHORS tab.

Seriocomic
Abdallah, twenties to thirties

Abdallah is addressing the audience. Later, we find out that it is his spirit that is on stage. He is full of the adventure of having emigrated to America.

ABDALLAH: *(accent)* I do very well for myself here. Three years in this new country and I turn a poor boy from Khartoum, me, into a businessman with much cash, as thick as a deck of playing cards. With my English, a language I must say almost as beautiful as my own, which I learn before coming here, with this language, I quickly learn to figure out things as soon as I come to this country with all its strange customs. Its different ways of doing things, and seeing the world. The different foods, the *huge* portions of food and the amazing size of buildings. As well as of course, to be honest, the fantastic cleavage of women I see everywhere. My God. Let me speak of this for a moment. What is in the water that so many women here are so admirable to look at. It gives me such pleasure to compliment a woman in English who passes me by on the street. To say, "Good morning to you, beautiful" so she understands. The rest, I might say to myself in my own language. But to be able to compliment in the language of your hosts, it makes a difference. So, in general, I have no problem fitting in. And finding a job right away. Odd jobs: busboy, dish washer, cleaning offices. I meet other people doing this, Sudanese, Koreans, Nigerians; and they recommend other jobs. Working at a grocery store, a laundromat. Meeting other nationalities, Guatemalans, Polish, Russians. I got to learn some Russian. I can say "piss off" in fluent Russian.

    (says it in Russian: "vati otsjuda")

And "kiss my ass" in Spanish

(says it in Spanish: "besame el culo")

And "park that behind right here, baby", in English. And in meeting all these people, I get to know them. And believe it or not, what they say about people is true, boring as it is: we are all basically, wonderfully the same. I think this is why there are so many quarrels. Because we see ourselves in the way other people act; and you know how hard we can be on ourselves. But that is not what I want to talk about, at least not in this way. I will talk of this by telling you how I got rich. Very rich. You see, in getting to know all these people, with the music of their different languages in my ear, I learnt all about the things they dream about and wanted. Services they need but don't know how to get because their English is not so good. And in knowing so many people, I knew for instance that what Carlos was looking for, Dimitri had; or what Nadif dreamed about getting cheaply I could arrange a special discount from Amina. And so on. Connecting people. For business. Becoming a middleman. Knowing how to do simple things for people who just arrive. And soon businesses learn of my skills and pay me to help with the immigrants who work for them. I make more money in this big city than I ever could in my home town. Arriving in a land filled with so many strangers, and enough strangeness in it it could make you cry sometimes, in spite of all this, I do great. And so I say, Abdallah, you have to give thanks to God. It is time you make the Hajj. And so I went. Happily. Because my heart had also been made rich by this journey. It made me feel so good that I could make such a difference in people's lives . . . . Unfortunately . . . the boat I was on that was carrying me across the Red Sea to Mecca, was too small for so many people . . . . And it sank.

Information on this playwright may be found at:
www.smithandkraus.com.
Click on the AUTHORS tab.

Dramatic
Tayyib, mid to late thirties

Tayyib, mid to late 30's, is speaking to Musa, He is trying to counsel him against dating an "American woman."

TAYYIB: Shut up and listen. I will tell you something, I found a woman early on. This American woman. Beautiful, sexy. In your fantasies you dream of a woman like this. And we were in love. We could not have been more so. We looked into each other's eyes and all the pieces of the world fit together. I believe in love; I do. But any love, it must—any love must have some common sense behind it. A solid ground for real feelings to take root. And not end after the first quarrels. But we, stupid in love, thought nothing could touch us. Because like all lovers we thought we were different. But by the end, everything was kicking our behinds. Everything. Small things, and very quickly. My speaking two languages for instance, and how she felt shut out when I invited my friends over and spoke in my own tongue. Or the smells from the kitchen when I cooked my food and how that made my sweat taste funny and could we eat "normal" food for once. And even that I went to the mosque, or rolled out my mat to pray at home. And all of these were charming to her in the beginning. Don't think they weren't. It was like a little spice for her, and for me, the different ways *she* did things. I loved it. But eventually, she began to miss home. Her idea of what home-life should be. And so did I. Musa:—You cannot be a foreigner twice in this country. When you are out here, you are a foreigner, but when you go home, you must be allowed to hang up your foreigner hat and be yourself. Do not mistake the woman who gives you pleasure with the woman who will surround you with things that feed you, in here. Gamila is a beautiful woman. *She* will make you feel at home. And without this home, this country will eat you up little by little. What happens to most lovers? One day you wake up and don't say good morning to the person you once adored. The only difference with us is the reasons that led to this. And the taste it left in my mouth. That I let someone make me feel more of a foreigner than I already was. Where I actually felt embarrassed to be who I was.

Information on this playwright may be found at:
www.smithandkraus.com.
Click on the AUTHORS tab.

Port Out, Starboard Home
Sheila Callaghan

Seriocomic
Johnny O, could be any age

In this speech, Johnny O, the captain of a mysterious themed cruise ship for spiritual renewal, addresses the passengers. Johnny O is aloof, ageless, and seems to exist out of time. The cruise's upcoming main event is some kind of unique spiritual ritual relating to a crew member named Maya and her baby. For now, the ritual is shrouded in secrecy, but Johnny O is slowly preparing the passengers for the spiritual journey they will undergo. In this speech, he calls their attention to the ship's crew, who are shadowy, wordless, yet ever-present.

JOHNNY O: Attention.
This is your cruise director
Jonnie O
Speaking
Are you all having a good time?
Don't forget Crown Bingo
Double Jackpots in the Casino
The Champagne Art Auction
The Captain's Welcome Reception
And all just before three PM!
But if you are saving up your energy for tomorrow's
MAIN EVENT, never fear.
PLENTY of lounging space by the pool!
And please don't forget to give a warm Crown Hello to
our guest of honor, Maya, and the small
one attached to her. They deserve your most special attention. But don't fret if you miss her!
You shall see her at your mandatory meeting. And if for
some reason your assigned time slot does
not suit your schedule, please see an event facilitator
immediately. There are multiple slots, and

we are happy to accommodate you. Once you receive
your slot number, please immediately
connect with those who have received the same number.
Bond, frolic, have fun! You will need to
build trust in one another. I cannot stress this enough.
If you have not attired yourself in your protective dining
enjoyment wear at this time,
please do so.
And now it is time for....
THE LUNCH BUFFET!!!!
>   *Everyone cheers.*
But before we launch
I want you to take a moment to thank your servers
These elegant humans, these dashing creatures
Hauling your bag
Pouring your beverage
Playing your song
Snapping your photo
Teaching your salsa
Hot-stoning your spine
Loading your plate
Mopping your vomit
These are not servants
These are gods
They hold you in the lowest regard
They look at your pasty faces, your sunburned thighs
Your stupid hats
Your rinky-dinks
Your pathos
And they bile themselves
Look upon them
Look upon them
as they pity you
>   *(JOHNNY O is a fire and brimstone preacher. His
>   speech goes on forever.)*
Yea, they prepare your lunch buffet
the stove is made ready
the griddle hottened

the flames do now rage and glow
the meats bubble and the oil spits
The glittering spatula is whet
and held over you as you round the corner
clutching your plate with your cavernous mouths
Your privilege and pansied ignorance makes you fools
Because you know not what you lack!
All you do is feed feed feed the endless vacuum of your
soul
With only a hazy recognition of your moral failings.
Until now.
So haste, my friends
Fall to your knees
Mop the perspiring toes of these Gods with your well-
conditioned hair
Worship them as is their due
They shall be happy to cater to your desires
From now until disembarkation
As they are the ambassadors of your transformation.
Enjoy your meal.

Dramatic
Daniel, mid-thirties

Daniel Milton, a renegade scientist, speculates to every-
one onstage, and the audience, about some frightening
scientific advances.

DANIEL: Something new from the drugstore. High-level
EMPATH drug,
> *(reading label)*

Vasopressin, Dopamine, Acetylcarnitine, Cobra Venom
Concentrate. Take sex—you do someone, you feel what
you're feeling and you feel what they're feeling. The drug
is in your saliva. Pass it on. A drop on the skin and they
feel what you feel, which is what you feel and what they
feel. Feedback loop is infinite, can't tell who's you and
who's who till the drug wears off at dawn . . . Or take a
dose and just sit quietly, look at a dead pine tree.
> *(DANIEL pulls something else from another pocket.*
> *This small bottle is glowing. He holds it up.)*

Nanobots. Little bio-chemical switcheroos. Drink me!
> *(He drinks it down, tosses it aside, begins to*
> *dance.)*

Few billion nanobots just took up residence in my brain
capillaries. Whooo! Remember, folks, eyes don't see,
fingers don't touch—the brain does it all. You don't experience diddley till the big boy gets the message. Johnny
Nanobot gets in there, and he's intercepting, changing,
inventing the message. Any damn way you want. You
program the little fuckers. It's Virtual Reality from inside,
a hundred percent equal to the so-called "real world"
in resolution and believability. Be someone else and be
somewhere else! You never know it's Johnny Nanobot,

'cause it's all there is. All and everything. You might burn out a few neurons, but what the hell. Hey, everybody gets theirs. Wonderful, wonderful world.

Dramatic
Kevin, forty-five

Kevin is speaking to Miles. (Kevin's speech is sprinkled with the unique patois that is used by older generations in Nonantum, Massachusetts.) Until this moment, MILES has believed that Kevin is his uncle.

KEVIN: Guess it was thirty years ago. Memorial Day weekend. Mike Venizia, divia mush, throws his annual party up at his house on Lake Winnipesaukee. That year they let me tag along because my brother Joey? *He's prom king.* I kid you not. Whole time I'm thinkin' "divia, why you here?" Older mushes treatin' me like I'm a punk. Older jivals givin' me the air.

Friday night gets rowdy by the kegger, and Joey, such a mamaluc, he makes his move. Announces to God and country he's takin' Caitie Donahue—the most quistya jival of all—out to one o' those islands in the lake, in Mikey's sailboat. About seven mushes grab canoes, sleepin' bags, belagers—make it a party. I gotta stay behind. I'm just a chabby.

Next day, I see 'em comin' back. Joey's paradin' around like he's cock o' the walk. "Aw jeez," I think. "What did that chuco do?" Saturday night, these divias wanna go to the packy, smoke hooch, pick fights with the New Hampster boys—Joey disappears with 'em all, braggin' 'bout how he jawled your mother. I'm left behind again, but this time, so is Caitie. She's laughin'—I'll never forget this—she says: it's what our English teacher, Sister Lois, would call a perfect metaphor. Goin' out there in the boat, Joey couldn't even get the *sail* up. No wind at his back, if you receive my meanin'. She had to start the motor just to get the boat to *move*, and by the time they get to the island, Joey's passed out. *The king is dead.* Outta pity she puts him in her sleepin' bag, while she gets eaten by mosquitoes. I told ya she was a kind person. But when Joey wakes up, he draws his own conclusions, and certainly isn't bashful with spreadin' the overchay to the mushes.

So try to picture it: divia mushes out raisin' hell, other jivals sleepin' upstairs—sound o' crickets, three-quarter moon over Winnipesaukee. And me, Kevin Colletti, heart poundin', applyin' calamine lotion to the quistya jival of quistya jivals: Caitie Donahue.

    Beat.

Maybe it was wrong all this time to let Joey think he was the father. But he had his own big mouth to blame. Who were *we* to change the story? And Caitie figured: he'd wanna take care o' things— he made all that wonga from the fish market. Maybe he'd pay for an abortion— but he said "Cuya moi, I won't do that." And may I say somethin', Miles? *That's the best thing Joey's never done.* We were young and careless, but we *were* in love. You can judge the, uh, literary merit of our feelings. You're the editor.

NOTE: there is a glossary of terms and pronunciations in the script, which may be obtained from the author's agent (see Rights & Permissions section in the back of this book).

Information on this playwright may be found at:
www.smithandkraus.com.
Click on the AUTHORS tab.

PRINCES OF WACO
Robert Askins

Dramatic
Jim, twenty

Jim's Daddy was a preacher. He preached in Texas. Jim's Daddy died. Jim is having trouble keeping it together. Somebody who isn't too smart asked him to speak at the funeral. To speak to a congregation whose secrets he knows and whose lies he hates. This is what he says.

JIM: I ain't wanna be here. I didn't wanna come but somebody . . . and Deacon Bradley saw me passin by and well . . . That's how come I'm dressed like this . . . I don't know how to do this. Seein everybody out there all teary eyed. All respectful. I don't . . . okay . . . He was a smart man. I can say that about him. Cause that's what we're supposed to do. Right? Say the good stuff. He was a smart man. He spoke with the voice of God . . . cause . . . cause . . . Fuck it. Why can't we be honest. Here in front of God why can't we be honest. I know where he hid his porn. He wanted to kill someone in Vietnam. He hated potato salad . . . all of your potato salad . . . He spoke with the voice of God cause it let him tell us all what pieces of shit we are. And we are. Brothers and sisters we are. Half of you have fucked Bill Fischer's wife. And everybody knows it. Everybody. This is what he saw sitting in these pews. Lust. Gluttony. Greed. Who won't Jim Kettler kill for a dollar. Ronnie Todd beats the shit outta his kids every Saturday and he comes here to get saved every Sunday.

(Jim bows his head. He raises it again.)
He wept in the night for a better world. He wept and wept and wept and in the morning Jesus come to him

and whispered in his ear: You save your water. JESUS
WANTED YOU TO.

*Information on this playwright may be found at:
www.smithandkraus.com.
Click on the AUTHORS tab.*

Dramatic
Rob, twenty

Rob was the co-pilot on the Enola Gay, the plane which dropped the A-bomb on Hiroshima. He is in Hollywood to appear on a segment of "This is Your Life,:" but he has fled the studio when he learned that also on the program will be the Hiroshima Maidens, women who were horribly disfigured by the bomb. He has come into a dive bar near the studio. Here, he is talking to May, the cocktail waitress about a dangerous incident which occurred before he became a member of the Enola Gay's crew.

ROB: I was always partial to more poetic names. I felt like if I was gonna go down in flames I wanted to be floating on something that wasn't the punch-line of a joke. My favorite one was "The Majestic." And she was just that. Not flying her made me nervy already. And then, right before I go, my Colonel tells me my regular navigator won't be coming with me. And to a pilot that's kinda like telling you your wife won't be coming with you on your honeymoon. So, I get into the cockpit with van Kirk, this annoying navigator, good at his job but a sour, little prick. And I'm sitting on the runway in "The Great Artiste," on what very well could be my last mission of the War, and I watch "Straight Flush" slip into the air, nice and easy. Same for my buddy Captain Bock's plane, "Bock's Car"—another joke name. The plane ahead of me was called "Strange Cargo." Just as she approached the runway, this grating sound started coming from her. And just like that, her bomb bay doors flew open! The pilot just slammed on his breaks and a 10,000 pound, bright orange blockbuster bomb lands right there on the runway. A few hundred feet from me and my crew. And I'm thinking to myself, this is how it's gonna end? Talk about a joke. Me and my crew had to stay put, not move an inch. And that's when I started singing, "London Bridge is Falling Down." The song just came out of my mouth and before I know it the whole crew is singing with me.

(singing)
"Build it up with Japs and Krauts. Japs and Krauts. Japs and Krauts . . . " We were singing like stupid kids while we watched firemen cover that bomb in foam. And we kept on singing when a crew of soldiers put shackles around that thing and winched it up, inch by inch. Took hours. They treated that bomb like it was the finest crystal.

Information on this playwright may be found at:
www.smithandkraus.com.
Click on the AUTHORS tab.

Seriocomic
Cooper, early twenties

Cooper, a charming but rather callow college student student, is telling his buds about his Plan for his life.

COOPER: Aww, you know, I'm taking my time . . . No, no. I mean this—college lasts 4 years thing. That was just a number some asshole picked out of thin air, you know? I'm young. I got time. It's like—I could stress out in my early 20's, and get work done and get that assignment in and write down what the professor says, but for what? To go work with my dad in a market like this? That doesn't sound like fun to me! And stressing out about shit is just going to take time off of my life. So—what? What's left? Two options we have. Option One—Pull a Davis. Don't get me wrong—a viable option. Do the work, make the grades, force an early life heart attack on yourself. Not judging, just saying. And there's option 2: The Cooper way. 4 years? Hell no. 5. 6. 6 and a half. And this way, I end up saving time. Why? Because people who opted for Option One work towards retirement, but the blood pressure and the anxiety and the extra bull shit stress decrease the chance of that 401K seeing the light of day. So us Option 2 guys—we'll cry at your funeral and mutter something about you being too young to die, but those extra 3 years I took in college, they turn into 20 or 40 extra years added to my vacation called—life. You want a beer?

Information on this playwright may be found at:
www.smithandkraus.com.
Click on the AUTHORS tab.

Dramatic
Johnson, twenty-one

*Johnson, a college student, is talking to his friend Davis,
another student, who is accused of having raped a girl at
a party.*

JOHNSON: Look this whole thing is a pretty big deal, alright? A big fuckin deal. I go to bed early every night.
I can count on one and a half hands the number of
times I've been drunk. I am a cautious mother fucker. I
haven't been able to breathe for all 21 years of my life
because I am trying, desperately, to become the man
that I want to be. And I'm sorry, but there are just too
many ways to fuck that up. And I won't allow it. Of
course I believe you, Davis. I know you. I know you
wouldn't do that. Not everybody knows you. Not the
dean. Not my parents. Not the press. And don't tell me
I'm not a good friend, because I am. I sit in class and
watch you doodle while I scramble to find a blank page
in my notebook. And it's like clockwork. I schedule
time before a test to help you before you even ask.
And I've never once bitched. I come to your house for
parties when you know full well that I hate parties. I
hate them. Not exaggerating. But I come because I'm a
good friend. And when Natalie dumped you, I was the
only one who didn't curse her out right away because I
knew you still loved her and didn't want to see her get
hurt, regardless of the shit she put you through. Why?
Because I am a good friend, Davis. You should know
that. So, I'm sorry if on the eve of my graduation from
college I don't want to be thrown into the midst of a
scandal, and knowing your parents and Leigh's back-
ground quite possibly a national scandal, regardless of

who's right or wrong. Be a good friend, Davis. Don't bring me down with you.

Information on this playwright may be found at:
www.smithandkraus.com.
Click on the AUTHORS tab.

RIDE THE TIGER
William Mastrosimone

Dramatic
Sam, fifty-two

*Frank Sinatra has been asked by Joseph Kennedy to per-
suade his friend Sam to help with the presidential campaign
of his son, Sen. John F. Kennedy. Sam is Sam Giancana, a
powerful Mafia boss who has strong political views.*

SAM: Frankie, first the Ruskies put up Sputnik One. Made
us look like a bunch o' fuckin' shoemakers. Then to rub
our nose in it, they put a mutt in orbit wit Sputnik Two.
Now the big slap in our face.
   (re: newspaper)
See this? First man in orbit. Yuri fuckin' Gagarin. They're
the champs, we're the chumps. And our guy didn't orbit
the earth like their guy. That five star Boy Scout in the
White House, he let the fuckin' Ruskies get so far ahead
of us. But the thing that burns my ass, all their science
the Ruskies kidnapped from the Nazis after the war. On
their own these Mongoloid fucks couldn't invent the
fuckin' firecracker. We're losin', Frankie, cuz they got
more thrust in their rockets to break through earth's, *como
si chiam'*, escape velocity. That's what they call it, the
rocket scientists. Hear what Khrushchev said? "We will
bury you." Like to meet that nickel-plated punk in a dark
alley and take a baseball bat to his Commie fuckin' head.
They stole the atomic bomb from us. They got a bigger
army than us. They got more ICBMs than us. Frankie,
more I.C.B.M.'s—but no 'frigerators. These fuckin' *schi-
vosos* can't even feed themselves. What do they got over
there? Cabbages, potatoes, borscht. No wonder they're
fuckin' miserable. That little bowling ball with arms and
legs Khrushchev, he's knockin' off these little countries

Lawrence Harbison

149

one after another. We need a guy wit' balls to put that Bolshevik fuck in his place. You play to win, you play to win. You don't give a shit how you do it. You play to win. Khrushchev, he plays to win. Somebody gets in his way, they go into a big fuckin' hole, nobody saw nothin'. He plays to win. Your guy don't play to win, this fuckin country mise well hoist the white fuckin' flag.

Information on this playwright may be found at:
www.smithandkraus.com.
Click on the AUTHORS tab.

Ride The Tiger
William Mastrosimone

Seriocomic
Sam, fifty-two

*Sam has become smitten with Judy, a young woman he
has spotted sunning herself by the pool at a Miami hotel.
Sam is Sam Giancana, the boss of the mob. Judy is Judith
Exner, formerly Frank Sinatra's girlfriend, who is now
having an affair with the President of the United States,
John F. Kennedy.*

SAM: Judy, look, you meet somebody, Hello, somebody,
Hello, How are you, Fine, and it's just words that tell
you nothin'. Because we're afraid to ask what we really
want to know. I wanna read the book of Judy. Who are
you? Where do you come from? How'd you grow up?
Do you like good wine and good food? Do you have a
good heart? Do you believe in God? Can you cook? Can
you do that new dance, the twist? Look at you. You're
perfect. Your nails. Your skin. Your hair. Your teeth.
Your jewelry. But who are you? I gotta get the skinny. I
wanna know about your folks, your first kiss, your boy-
friends, your girlfriends, do you like chocolate, vanilla,
strawberry? And while we're at it, why don't you read
my book? I'm a book too. You only saw my cover. Read
a few pages. Get to know me. Let me get to know you.
Let's make some rules here. I don't make no moves on
you. I don't touch you. You're the boss. Okay? As St.
Francis of Hoboken once said—
    (singing)
"Let's take it nice and easy, it's gonna be so easy, for us to
fall in love . . . " You remind me of my beautiful mansion
up the road in Palm Beach. Gorgeous beachfront. More
rooms than a hotel. Lawns. Fountains. Bougainvillea.

And you're tellin' me in all the mansion of Judy you can't find a place for me in your life? Not in all those rooms? Not in the basement? Not in the broom closet? What do you think I want? That ain't it. You make me forget all my pride. I get tired of the games between men and women. I can be myself around you. No games. No pretend. That's what I want. Your company. This. What we have right now. Talk. Friendship. Nothin' more. You know, Judy, after my wife passed, never thought I could feel anything for anybody. But life played a big surprise when I met you. I wanna take you to my place in Palm Beach. When you're ready. And I wanna cook for you. You like pasta vongole? Pasta and clams. Judy, when I make pasta vongole, people fall down. But they get up again cuz they want seconds. That's all I want. The pleasure of your company.

Information on this playwright may be found at:
www.smithandkraus.com.
Click on the AUTHORS tab.

Dramatic
Gupta, Indian, thirties

Gupta is speaking to Priya. Her father has arranged for Gupta to marry her, but Gupta has come to Priya to ask her himself.

GUPTA: The ocean is one of the great joys of life they say. I beg your pardon. I did not mean to startle you, Priya. The ocean? To plunge in. Nothing holding you in place. Floating freely. Heaven! But America? It is overrated, you know. The romantic choice for the greedy. Make a fortune, they think. But India's the place to make one's fortune today. We have all the opportunity. That's why the Americans are coming to us. Though America's science is very good. Very good. If you want to cross the ocean, go to Africa. Yes, HIV/AIDS, I know. But not by the ocean, not on their beaches. Dar, Maputo, Durban— extraordinarily beautiful I'm told. I have family in Africa, you know. I've been saying I should visit them. It would be ideal for a special holiday. The kind a couple takes to celebrate their life together. Do you know what I say to my relatives whenever they tell me theirs is the most beautiful place in the world? Do you know, Priya? I say there is nothing more beautiful than what I gaze upon right here. In our little town, in our little clinic. What I see every day. The people with whom I work. The people for whom I care deeply. The people who bring me joy each and every moment of each and every day. And of course our wondrous lake. You know I am speaking about you. I am so pleased to be here with you, my Priya. So pleased. My heart would lie down at your feet if it could. It would kiss your lovely ankles and stroke your calves. No, no. Let me say what I have to say. I have come with a purpose. I think you know this. And though it is a joyous occasion, I struggle to express what I feel. Priya, our families are the oldest and most prominent in this town. We have grown up together, sharing everything in our lives. And these last three years with you beside me every day in clinic—when the end of work came each day and we returned to our own homes, our own beds, I said no, no this is not right. This is not what our lives were meant to be. Please. Just this one question. Allow me to ask and to hear your beautiful answer. I know I do not have to. Your father has spoken of the bond already. But it is your words I long to hear. Your heart against mine. Your soul and mine like the oceans of the world, separate in name but flowing together all as one in their physical incarnations.

Information on this playwright may be found at:
www.smithandkraus.com.
Click on the AUTHORS tab.

Dramatic
Francisco, late teens, Latino

Francisco is speaking to Tony. Francisco's a computer geek who works as a kind of hacker. Tony's come to Francisco for help finding a woman he met on line, but now has doubts about going through with it because Francisco, who's young and not exactly professional, isn't what Tony expected. Francisco's trying to convince Tony to let him do the job.

FRANCISCO: I'm playing with you. You wanna find her, right? Real bad, right? I bet she's hot. She hot? She put her picture up? Fucking guarangas and shit? The flesh so ripe you can taste it? Come on, man, I'm shitting you. Bullshit boy talk, you know. But I can see that's not your game. You know how it is, right? You can't trust most of that cyber shit. Not that I wanna lose your business. People are fuckin with each other all the time. It's old news. I can see you're straight, man. I mean full of the force, nothing on the dark side. People are good and all that shit. I can get down with that. She may be P. Cruz with the heart of Mother Teresa and not give a shit about your wallet. Who knows? But look, you'll never know if you walk away, now. You have to do this, you said. So follow your heart now, man. It got you this far. It's only a little green. Find out what her deal is. It's gonna change your life one way or the other. Look, I can see you're a proper dude. Upstanding member of the community and all that. Your heart, your heart has been touched. Like never before. You can't think of anything else, not work, not food, not your friends. Your fingers touch the keys and it's like her skin ignites you. Your body quivers as the words fill the screen. It's like her soft breath brushes your cheek with each sentence. Flickering letters pulse with your chest. You want to kiss every word. You want to burn the screen into your body. There can't be anything between the two of you any more. Nothing. Just her and you together. And that's why you're here. We all need somebody, man. Let me help you. Let me put you together so the electricity that binds you is snappin direct. No wires, no glass, no distance. Flesh to flesh. Soul to soul. One.

Information on this playwright may be found at:
www.smithandkraus.com.
Click on the AUTHORS tab.

Samuel J. and K.
Mat Smart

Comic
J, twenty-nine

Samuel J tells his friend Samuel K about a situation he encountered at the local Dunkin' Donuts.

J: I'm not ready for anything! I mean, I go to the Dunkin' Donuts drive-thru on my way out to Lisle in the morning and I'm never even ready to order. "May I take your order?" Whoop—my mind goes blank. I know I'm hungry, but do I want a doughnut, a muffin, or a breakfast sandwich? And then what kind of doughnut?—what kind of muffin? Sometimes I have to say, "you know what? I'm just gonna park and come in." I was in there yesterday and there was this guy complaining to the woman about how she cut his bagel. He was like "you never cut my bagel in half—it's always like so-not-down-the-middle—how hard is it to cut something down the middle?" And this like sixty-year-old guy is going off and I'm just like—not in a rude voice, like in a nice voice—nice-ish voice— "Dude, maybe you should just make your own bagel at home and cut it the way you want." He's like, "what'd you say to me?" I'm like, "She's got ten people in line, it's a bagel, it's not worth getting upset about." And he's like, "mind your own business." And I was like—in a not-so nice-ish voice—"Well, sir, it's people like you that make the world a shitty place. It's people like you that make me want to live on a deserted island." And he was like, "Would you like to say that to me again outside?" And then I was like—to this *sixty*-year-old dude—"Okay, grandpa, let's do this!" But then the woman working there was like, "Please gentlemen!—it's okay—I am happy to cut the bagel any which way—it's my job— it's okay." And both me and the guy shut up. And I just stare at the floor. I wanted to go cry in my car, but I was like—if I leave now, how am I ever going to come back into the Dunkin' Donuts that is right on the way to the Arboretum?

Dramatic
Abel, late forties

*Abel is Vera's abusive husband in Canyon, Texas, and the
man from whom she and Mike her newlywed are fleeing,
but in this play of memory and the replay of memory, he
takes on a mythic stature. He becomes larger than life as
he embodies all their doubts and fears about their ability
to raise their forthcoming baby. As he says, "Think of me,
I'm here." Abel is both real and unreal, and he uses a language that is heightened with a sense of manifest destiny
and its own twisted poetry. In the scene from which this
speech is taken, he appears just as they learn that they are
pregnant with their baby Cristina. Abel comes to lay claim
to the unborn infant.*

ABEL: We always wanted a baby, baby. Since forever, I've
    been prepping for the comin' of life. Before I even knew
    Vera, I bought a house and set one room aside and even
    painted it pink. 'Cause we knew, didn't we? She had to
    be a girl. And didn't we try to bring forth? Time after
    time, I did my level best for the sake of our future, but
    you just couldn't conceive. You seemed to be an infertile
    specimen. I started to doubt the power of my own pecker.
    My potency came into question and started me down
    a road I couldn't hardly bear. Who was I if not Abel?
    Who was you if not mother of my pups? Then I found
    your pills taped under the bed. Hidden away so damned
    good, a drug-sniffing dog would no sooner find my pot
    than your cute little stash. But I found it. And I knew that
    my junk was potent and true, brimming with a legion of
    red-blooded little Abels ready to blow you up. I learned
    the power of a woman's lie was no match for me. I'm
    sorry that hell and doom rained on you night and day for

a while, and I'm sorry about your teeth, but you needed that poison pounded outa you. You are Vera the Woman of Abel and that Child is our Day-to-Day and this Mike is Destiny's Loser. 'Cause The Hootchie-Kootchie to End All Hootchie-Kootchie cannot be denied. I got a baby in you yet. UH! UH! UH!

THE SOAP MYTH
Jeff Cohen

Dramatic
Silver, forties to fifties

*Daniel Silver, a Holocaust scholar, works for an organi-
zation which documents the atrocities perpetrated by the
Germans. Annie Blumberg, a young journalist, has come to
him to advocate for an elderly Jewish man who claims to
have documentary proof that the Nazis made soap from human corpses. Silver has rejected his claim. Here's why.*

SILVER: There was a Dr. Rascher in the SS. The air force
wanted to know what would happen to human beings at
extremely high altitudes with extremely low levels of ox-
ygen. At Dachau, Rascher did medical experiments that
approximated conditions at altitudes of almost ten miles.
He took a relatively healthy 37 year-old Jew and watched
how long it would take him to die. He took meticulous
notes. He was so excited by this that he called in another
physician as a witness. This is what they observed. After
four minutes the experimental subject begins to perspire
and to wiggle his head. After 5 minutes cramps occur.
Between 6 and 10 minutes breathing increases in speed
and the experimental subject becomes unconscious. From
11 to 30 minutes breathing slows down to three breaths
per minute. At 30 minutes, the test subject breathes his
last shallow breath and dies. Ms. Blumberg, how do we
know this happened? Because Rascher was so *proud* of
what he'd done that he sent a letter to the chief of the SS
Himmler in April of 1942 detailing all of this. We have
that letter. That is evidence. That is proof. The air force
conducted experiments on people who were severely
chilled or actually frozen—subjects were forced to sit
naked in tanks of ice water for periods up to 3 hours.
Others were kept naked outdoors in the dead of winter

in bitterly cold temperatures. The victims screamed with pain as their bodies froze. The doctors took notes. We have those notes. There were malaria experiments. Over a thousand inmates were infected by mosquitoes or were injected with malaria. There were mustard gas experiments. Inmates were purposefully wounded and then those open wounds were doused with mustard gas. More? Subjects were deliberately wounded and those wounds infected with various bacteria—streptococcus, gangrene, and tetanus. Then, their blood vessels were cut and tied off like hoses to stop blood circulation. This was meant to approximate battlefield injuries and, to make it more authentic, ground glass and wood shavings were forced into the wounds. Ms. Blumberg, I have a daughter about your age. I take no pleasure in subjecting you to this. We who are historians of this period try to remain detached from it. We try to keep our distance from the personal stories we are telling. It may not be the right thing to do, but it is our way of surviving it. When a man like Milton Saltzman comes calling, my detachment collapses. I see his rage, the numbers tattooed on his arm, I see it in his eyes. And you're not sure you can make him understand the *intricacies* of the arguments that we use to dismiss his claim. You're not sure you fully understand it yourself. After all, there is the Nuremberg testimony on soap. There were exhibits of soap for four decades. Histories of the holocaust were written and soap included without caveat. And then the Deniers spend fortunes debunking claims such as this. And yet they present no evidence, they merely raise doubts. And the next thing you know, Holocaust scholars have reclassified soap. I *do* understand. But what I can say to you, and I hope that *you* can understand *me,* is whether it really matters in light of *all* of the inexplicable acts that Nazi Germany perpetrated. The history of humanity is a history of inhuman acts. I have a passion for chronicling that inhumanity—yes, at the end of the day, I too, along with Esther Feinman and all of our colleagues, are dreamers. We are romantics. We are optimists. By telling the stories of our inhuman history, we believe with a deep passion that one day, people will stop. One day they will say—*why are we doing this? Where does it get us? We have the capacity to stop.*

Information on this playwright may be found at:
www.smithandkraus.com.
Click on the AUTHORS tab.

Seriocomnic
Kellar, late teens

Kellar, a marine, is trying to write a letter to his sweetheart. He asks a fellow marine—a woman—for help.

KELLAR: It's just that I get nervous and I start talking and talking and I can't stop. It's how I work things out and I've been writing this letter over and over and over—to Lauren—and I just can't get it right. She's gonna get this letter and just barf everywhere—she'll be swimming in barf this letter will make her barf so much—

(KELLAR crumples up the piece of paper and throws it)
(still, quietly throughout)

I mean, she is so mad at me. The last night before I left—I took her out to a really nice dinner at this really nice place—it was like French—well, kind of this French fusion place—it was awesome. It was twice as fancy as the place Lauren and I went to for prom. And I got her roses. And bought her this bracelet that was four hundred thirty-two bucks after tax—like if you take all the stuff I've bought for any girlfriend ever before and *combine* it all—it doesn't equal four hundred thirty-two bucks. So I give her this bracelet and I think she's gonna freak out like in those diamond commercials—even though this didn't have any diamonds—and be all, "I love you, I love you, every kiss begins with K"—or some shit—but she just starts *crying*. Like bawling. And for a moment I'm like—she's so happy she's crying! Awesome, right? Wrong. She thought it was gonna be a ring! And I'm like "We're way too young to get married" and she's all "You're going to war tomorrow and you think you're too young to get married?" And we left everything a total mess—I don't even know how we left things and so I'm trying to write this stupid letter to say—

(KELLAR gets the crumpled up letter and uncrumples it. He reads)

"Baby, just because I'm not ready to get married, doesn't mean I don't love you." Barf!

She's gonna be swimming in barf. Do I just need to propose to her? Should I just write: "Lauren, will you marry me?"

(He writes it.)

Agh! That doesn't look right!

(KELLAR crumples up the letter again)

I just wanted to get like a female perspective on it, Powell. What should I do, ma'am?

You're always reading those letters. Thought maybe you could give me some pointers.

Please.

Comic

Orlando, fifteen, Hispanic or African American

Orlando is a 15 year old foster child and he is addressing a 65 year old suicidal playwright named Saul Sunshine. They are strangers but the boy has just saved the man from jumping off the roof. Now, as they are become acquainted, Orlando is telling the Saul a few facts about his own life.

ORLANDO: I like to design clothes for ladies. The kids at school call me a fag and we mix it up a lot. Sometimes they beat the shit out of me. Sometimes I beat the shit out of them. But if I get my new mom—if my new mom gets *me*—she's gonna put me in a private school—you know, where the teachers outnumber the students. (*pause*) Hey, you got a minute? I can talk to you because you're gonna be dead before the sun comes up. Right? You ain't gonna tell no one; right? Promise? Cross your heart? I think maybe I'm gay. Not that I ever did anything about it. And like I don't have crushes on guys. Except this one guy, Bobby! He's a white guy—but he's cool. I like to hang out with him. Like he's my buddy! Or maybe he's like my big brother. But maybe he's more than that. I don't know, man. There's this girl, Samantha. She's real tall. Laughs a lot! Like her laugh feels me up inside . . . here. I like her a lot. I have fantasies about her—you know—like making out with her. But I never made out with anyone. So I don't know. I think, when the time comes, if the time *ever* comes, maybe I'm gonna be . . . you know . . . But I like girls. I like to design dresses for girls. Does that make me gay? Nobody calls me a fag, not to my face, because if they do, I'm gonna bust their ass.

The Taint Of Equality
Duncan Pflaster

Comic
Adrian, thirties to forties

The Taint of Equality, or I Want Your Sex concerns Adrian and Javier, a gay couple who don't believe in Gay Marriage, since it is based on heterosexual models, which they consider inherently unequal. Despite their stand, everyone they know keeps referring to them as married, so they decide to each go out and have an affair to show how free and unrestricted they are. In this scene, Adrian has met P.J., a dopey young straight man whose girlfriend is out of town, and who has invited Adrian back to his place.

ADRIAN: Look, I've had enough bi-curious straight guys in my life to choke a horse. You all think that even if you have a girlfriend, that gay sex doesn't count. That it doesn't mean anything if a dude just goes down on you. Well, I will have you know that it *does* mean something. I have a boyfriend who I love very much; we have an open relationship, we can sleep around with whoever we want. The problem is respect, P.J., if that *is* your real name. I actually left the house today with the explicit intention of getting laid. The problem is that I don't want to be part of your weird little fantasy life. I have my *own* fantasies, thank you, and they do not include you. Let me give you a little history lesson, kid. Back in the 1940s through the 1970s, gay dudes were more than happy to blow any straight guys who were willing to "allow us" to service them. For young sailors on leave who didn't want to spend money on prostitutes, fags were the free option. A lot of gay slang comes from the hooking world because of that. "Tricks", "trade", "cruising". And this was all due to our self-hatred, due to society keeping us down. We didn't think we could find, or even deserved, love. Well, P.J., things have changed. There's visibility. We know who we are. America knows who we are. So we're no longer as grateful for the phallic crumbs that horny straight men deign to drop in our path. We're not mere sucking machines, useful vacuum cleaners, anymore. We want respect, we want equality. Certainly there can be a certain filthy romance to be found, in wallowing in that sort of gratis meretricious fellatio, but we have risen above it. Or at least *I* have, and I feel we all should. So you can put away your wang, my boy. I shan't be sucking on it.

Information on this playwright may be found at:
www.smithandkraus.com.
Click on the AUTHORS tab.

The Tiger Among Us
Lauren Yee

Comic

Pao, twenty-three. Asian (Hmong) American

Pao, an Asian American, talks to a class of 7th graders about the Hmong people.

PAO: Okay. So. My name's Pao. You can call me Mr. P. That's cool, too, if you want. Right, Ms. G? Okay. So. Hmong. Everyone, they wanna know what Hmong is. Everyone around here, they like, what the fuck— 'scuse my mouth—But they like, fuck, it's cold up in here and we're freezing our asses off and there're all these tropical Asians showing up. And they're like, I thought we were all blond up in here. So I can tell you what Hmong is but it's like real secret. Like Imma kill you secret, No shit. Okay, so Hmong, we come from a bunch of different countries We ain't got no, like, Hmong country I don't know why. Guess 'cause nobody likes us. Which I get—I don't like me either, story of my life—And we're from all over. We're in China. And then fucking Chinese—no offense, nobody's Chinese?—Fucking Chinese, they're like fuck you. So we go down to Laos and fucking Laos—or Laotians—They're also like fuck you and they try to kill us. BUT THEY CAN'T! 'Cause we're TROPI-CAL SURVIVORS! With the TIGERS and LIONS and flesh-eating MONKEYS! We hunt those dudes for breakfast. We eat tiger for breakfast! Tony the Ti-ger kind! 'Cause we're CIA motherfuckers! You ever hear this shit? About how the American government recruited Hmong guys to fight the Viet Kong for them, 'cause I guess Asian-on-Asian violence is cheaper. OH! And we eat snake. For the protein. We bite the shit out of them headfirst and swallow the whole thing up.

They're like noodles to us: Snake ramen. That's our
Thanksgiving dinner. People're like, "oh, yeah, turkey,"
And we're like "oh, yeah, snake." Naw, I'm just playing!
We don't really eat snake.

Dramatic
Ed, early thirties

Ed is speaking to Amy, with whom he had a passionate three-night stand following their first meeting, after which she disappeared, taking his wallet with him. He has tracked her down to her childhood home in New Jersey where she is in the process of breaking some very bad news to her family

ED: You don't have to look so surprised. You knew I'd come back. That's me, right?—the guy who comes back. I mean, I'm the guy who tracked you down—all the way to fucking NEW JERSEY, after you disappeared, with my WALLET. Yeah, I don't know if you heard, Sir, but your daughter's thief. It's really disappointing, you know. She seemed so . . . full of promise. I should have known. I'm a teacher, you know. 9th grade English. Now, those kids are full of promise—bright faces, deep trust funds. I used to think I was full of promise too, but then, I've never been a great judge of character. But your daughter . . . . I think she's got something. Or at least she better, if she keeps going around like this. Cause this is a lot to put up with if not. So, okay—HUGE mistake to come here! No need to mention it—I'm pretty clear where I went wrong. Guess you're not the only one with some serious impulse control issues, HUH? But did you really have to use me as your buffer? Or—not even a buffer—more like one of those blow-up bumpers that line the gutters at a bowling alley—yeah. You know— just the thing you bounce off of on your way to wherever you're trying to get. Maybe next time, when you have some kind of major life-changing information to impart to your family, maybe don't rope your new friend into it. JUST A THOUGHT. Amy, you haven't realized this yet, but MOST people are miserable. MOST people are terrified. You're not the only one. Look at your sister. Look at your Dad-no offense. But they don't seem like happy-go-lucky folks to me. And clearly neither am I. But maybe if one time you didn't walk out on something when you got scared, you might actually end up as the exception to the rule. And wouldn't you be lucky. We're all a mess, Amy. So get over yourself.

Information on this playwright may be found at:
www.smithandkraus.com.
Click on the AUTHORS tab.

Comic
Zero, twenties to thirties

Zero is talking to his roommate, Chris, and his room-mate's girlfriend, Leah, about this crazy event he saw on his way home

ZERO: *(setting it up like a joke)* Alright check it out: I'm walking home a couple blocks from here, and in the middle of an intersection are these two guys: a taxi driver and a clown. A clown—baggy polka-dot pants, fluffy red hair, big red nose—Bozo the Clown. The taxi rear-ended Bozo's car, which for the record is regular-sized, and Bozo's like, "I have two more payments left!", and the taxi driver's like, "Fuck you, you clown." They start pushing each other, and the dude riding in the taxi—stock-broker type: slicked hair, shined shoes—he gets out of the taxi and is like, "I have an important meeting at so and so," and the driver and clown are like, "Fuck you, money." So they're all shoving and what-not, when I swear to God, a second clown comes out of the car. His wife, 'cause she's like, "Let go of my husband, you motherfuckers!", and as she's walking toward them, she trips over her big red shoes, like it's an act, but it's not an act, and she bites it hard, man, she's bleeding, and the taxi driver and stock broker are laughing at her, so Bozo punches the driver, and bride of Bozo kicks the broker in the dick. By now there's a sizeable crowd. Cars stop honking, people's heads are poking out of windows; time ceases to exist. The driver grabs for the clown's nose as the clown's strangling the driver with his suspenders; the wife's attacking the broker with her shoes while the broker's searching for his missing cufflink. The entire city block's begging for more.

    (beat)

The wife clown goes to her trunk and takes out a tire iron, 'cause the trunk's open from the rear-ending, right? She starts beating the broker with it. Hard, like she's swinging for the fences. Again and again, until the broker stops moving, until she's sure he's dead. The block was silent.

(pause)

I tried to stop her. But I was so, stunned, so caught off guard, my brain couldn't talk right to my feet. And then it was over.

(beat)

I'm shuffling home, trying to make sense of what I just saw, when something miraculous happens. I get an idea. It came from that quiet voice inside you, you know? The one that tells you truths you hate to hear so you ignore it? Well I couldn't ignore this, because the idea is so brilliant in its simplicity yet at the same time so impossible to fully conceive, it has to be inspired. Right now I'm more concerned about its execution. Ever since I was a kid, I've been told I'm capable of greatness, and I believe I am but, I'm still looking for what I'm *good* at, you know? Where I belong. Suddenly I have an idea, and the voice is linking it to events in my life and how they intersect and connect. As to how to get it done, and what it all means, I've been given only fragments, puzzle pieces, and a promise: put the pieces together, and when the enlightenment comes—Seven days, man. In seven days I'll know how I fit in. In seven days the world as we know it will end.

Seriocomic
Boy, teens

A teenaged boy is talking about a sex scandal at his school to an older woman he has met at the bus stop.

BOY: I had a teacher just like you. Mrs. Bl- wait you might know her. She had sex with a senior at my school Matt Hoop- he killed himself, it was in the paper. She got pregnant, Mrs. Bl- and she wanted to keep it because she was—how old are you again? Doesn't matter. She was much older than you and she didn't think there was any way, I mean there probably wasn't, this was her shot, it wasn't that she was ugly, she had dated this French guy, I don't know his real name, we called him Pierre, and they had been together for like 10 years, he didn't believe in marriage, maybe his father had fucked around, like Mitterrand, so he didn't believe in it. Pierre was either against having kids because of coming from a broken home, or just sterile, and then Mrs. Bl-, the teacher, when she turned 40, he left her, just went back to France, or met someone else, Tim Ross' mom didn't know for sure, anyway Pierre was suddenly gone and the teacher was suddenly 40 and crying all the time in class which was just embarrassing for the kids, it was so pathetic, and as a result we had like, as a class, the lowest A.P. French scores in the county. So it was like torture, every word she said was part of a conversa-tion with Pierre she would never have again, just bleh, bleh, bleh, blub, blub, blub all the time, I even went to the principal to get her fired, or sent on sabbatical till she got her shit together, not because I loved French so much, though I'm pretty good at it, "On n'apprend pas aux vieux singes a' faire des grimaces" (that's a french proverb), but no, I wanted her fired because it was just so disgusting the sob fest, and then, so, when she got pregnant and it was Matt Hoop—who was only in AP French because his dad was an undertaker and had like a chain of funeral homes, started with nothing but a shovel and a pair of black pants, put himself through Wesleyan, he was determined Matt would go to Wesleyan too, (but then Matt was a legacy so it shouldn't have been that hard, maybe he just needed an AP attended on his admissions,) anyway Matt got like straight F's, he was always zonked out in the back of class, Zoloft probably, all in black like his dad, but ironically, I think, to piss his dad off, but so that's why—I mean I thought it even before I heard Tim Ross' mom say it—why Mrs. Bl- chose Matt to get pregnant by, because Matt would never learn to say shit in French, not merde. But then, when she told him she was keeping it? Matt killed himself in that crazy way . . . Come on, it was on TV, you don't even own a TV? Self-entombment. That's what he died by, self-entombment. He buried himself alive . . . It was kinda genius. There was a funeral that his dad was handling and he just swapped himself for the guy who was being buried. It was a closed casket deal, the dead guy, the already dead guy, Mr. Quinn I think, had died of some horrible like wasting disease, like Ebola of the head, and Matt's dad was like, "I can spruce him up and you can have the open casket but it'll cost you an arm and a leg to fix his face", and the Quinn family, they were Catholic and poor, not unrelatedly, and Mrs. Quinn, formerly Fleischer, was still kinda young so maybe she wanted to save a little heading into the second chapter of her life, not Tim Ross' mom's favorite, Mrs. Quinn nee Fleischer, so they went closed casket, but then when Mr. Quinn, or maybe it was O'Keefe, anyway when he was found in the woods by the road looking even more wasted, half eaten by woodlen creatures and all, everyone wondered who they had just buried, cause the coffin definitely had a body in it, it was heavy. Imagine it, Matt had to lay so still . . . . So when they dug up the casket, it was too late of course, he'd suffocated, or just, I don't know what kills you in self-entombment, dehydration maybe, but at some point he had changed his mind because it was a mess in there, he'd torn at the insides of the lid, all the lining, the stuffing was torn out, and it stank of course because you lose control of your functions when you die, you literally lose your shit, but it was also supposed to be beautiful with him all covered in ripped out white stuffing—like he was laying in a cloud, or a bath of angel feathers.

Information on this playwright may be found at:
www.smithandkraus.com.
Click on the AUTHORS tab.

Comic
Boy, a teen

The Boy is talking to a middle aged woman who has just bought him some beer. She has also bought a bag of Doritos.

BOY: *(He eats a chip.)* You know what I like with Cool Ranch, any Dorito really, as opposed to like a Sun Chip? Or a, I don't know, regular tortilla chip? The flavor dust that gets stuck to your fingers when you bite your chip. See? With Cool Ranch it's like, a blue and gold flavor dust. It's not really the color of ranch dressing. Maybe it's a metaphor: "Cool Ranch" . . . But then look at this: so like, you lick it off, the flavor dust,
    (He licks his fingers.)
Voila. But then when you go for the next chip, your fingers are like wet and sticky,
    (He eats another chip.)
so more flavor dust sticks to your fingers, so you lick em again, and your fingers get wetter and stickier, so there's gonna be more flavor dust, there's gonna be more licking, and eventually it'll just like coat your fingers, your tongue and lips get all coated too, and who knows eventually if the licking is actually cleaning your fingers, or just shellacking on more layers of pasty flavor dust. It's just like this passing back and forth of smoosh that's losing flavor. It's just this cleaning which isn't even tasting anymore, this cleaning that's only making a bigger mess. It's a negative feed back cycle. And the chip, the start of the whole thing, is like beside the point. Do you think *that's* a metaphor? Is, like, the chip our Life, the flavor dust our dreams, the fingers reality, they moosh

together, and then your mouth is like death?

(He licks his fingers.)

Or maybe the chip is your heart, the flavor dust is love, the fingers are heartbreak, and then time just gobbles them up?

(He bites a chip.)

Wait, no, what if the chip is the soul, the flavor dust is magic, the fingers what you do with your soul, and the mouth Deep Space . . . or Oblivion, or whatever that massive thing is which doesn't even know the world exists or we exist or that existence exists, that Vastness which is deafeningly neutral, neither good nor bad, just there, just true, just bigger than thoughts can think, and eyes can see, and mouths can say, and when you think about God, who no one should really think about, look what happened to Job who was a good guy, and always tried to be good, and God said, "You think you know me? You think you know what I want?" And then he bent Job over and fucked him so hard Job was like, "Ok! I get it, I get it," and God was like, "What? What do you get?" and Job was like, "I get that I don't get it, I won't get it, I can't get it, I get that there is nothing to get, there is only God, and He can fuck you up the ass whenever he wants to!" and God came in Job and blew out Job's brains and humankind has never thought of God, or conceived of the enormity of God since, because the part of our brains that could was blown away that day; *that* God, the real God, who we don't dare know the omniscience of, the omnipotence of, the plan, the rules of, *that* God, if He does exist, is only a blue flavor dust speck in the mouth of the True Vastness. We do not matter. More likely we are anti-matter. More likely it's not a metaphor. Most likely it's just a Cool Ranch Dorito.

Information on this playwright may be found at:
www.smithandkraus.com.
Click on the AUTHORS tab.

VANYA AND SONIA AND MASHA AND SPIKE
Christopher Durang

Comic
Spike, twenties

Spike is a vapid but extremely good looking aspiring actor whose girlfriend Masha is a famous movie star twice his age. She has encouraged him to tell her sister Sonya and her brother Vanya about a recent audition, and about how he recently changed agents.

SPIKE: So I was auditioning for the spin off series *Entourage 2*. And it has a different set up because in this one there's an up and coming actor who's starting to make it big in the movies, but he's played by somebody else, so the implication is it's another character. His name is Bradley Wood, and he's the lead. And in *this* version, his entourage is this old dame who's his agent, and this young guy on coke who's his manager, and his best friend from high school who's a girl who has a crush on him but she has this disease that gives her convulsions so she can never kiss anybody, cause she gets convulsions. And I live next door to a rabbi who's played by Judd Hirsch. But he's not on every week. Okay, and he's been having an affair with his older agent lady, but he's thinking of moving on to another agent. So the scene is between Bradley Wood and his lady agent. Okay he comes into the room, and the manager is there. Hey, good looking. How's tricks? Who told you that? Hey, don't cry. Come on, give me a smile. Besides it's not definite. Well . . . yeah, it's true, I did meet with some agents at CAA. I thought they were real impressive. I mean, they can call up Sandy Bullock, they can call up Julia Roberts. You gotta face it, you don't know that caliber of person. What?

(he listens)

What about loyalty? What about my career? What about my getting ahead? Yeah, I know you put in a lot of time with me. But I put a lot time in with you too. And I don't know . . . I think I might like CAA better. What?

(listens)

Oh, that. Well, yeah, just cause I go to another agent doesn't mean we have to stop sleeping together occasionally. Well I think it's occasional. I mean I sleep with other people too. I want to be successful, I can't just sleep with one old broad all the time. Oh, I'm sorry, don't cry. I think of "old broad" as a term of affection.

(listens)

Oh yeah? Well fuck you!

Information on this playwright may be found at:
www.smithandkraus.com.
Click on the AUTHORS tab.

WELCOME TO MY HEAD
Sam Bobrick

Comic,
Chuck, mid-thirties

Chuck Bradley addresses the audience explaining that being an agent isn't as easy as it looks and then goes into detail.

CHUCK: A lot of people have asked me, what does it take to be a writers agent besides a four thousand dollar Armani suit, a fifteen hundred dollar pair of Gucci alligator shoes with a matching belt, a three hundred and fifty dollar Hugo Boss shirt, a two hundred dollar Hermes tie, a hundred and thirty five dollar pair of Versace cashmere and silk socks and a seventy five dollar Rolex watch which is a knock off, but you'd never know. Well, first of all, being a writer's agent isn't as easy as it looks. You don't just sit around all day at a desk looking good. There are a lot of other important ingredients in the mix and none of them should be overlooked. The first ingredient is lunch. Chances are, if you're an important agent, you didn't get to the office until after eleven thirty. Well, it's crazy to think you can conduct business all day on an empty stomach. I tried it once, it doesn't work. The growling will keep you awake for hours. So the number one ingredient is lunch. Ingredient number two. It is absolutely mandatory that when going to lunch, you take someone in the business with you, like a producer or a director. This serves a twofold purpose. A, you'll be able to charge the meal to your company and B, you will eat at a much better restaurant then if you were paying for it yourself. Should by any chance they want to discuss business, which is in itself rare, you make a mental note not to invite them ever again. Lunch was invented to be enjoyed. Since you are a writer's agent, every now and then it might be a good idea to take a writer with you. I would not recommend this too often as they are a very, very gloomy bunch and being with one too long will cause you to have a very, very gloomy day and who needs that. Okay, ingredient number three. Phone calls. Since ninety five percent of your clients will be out of work with nothing better to do, you will be deluged daily by their phone calls. So here's the formula for that. The first phone call, have your assistant inform them that you're meeting with a producer about their script and you'll get back to them. The second phone call, have your assistant inform them that you're meeting with a director about their script and you'll get back to them. Their third call have your assistant put them on hold for twenty minutes and if they're still there when you pick up, don't blame yourself. Just remember you tried your best. Now as a writer's agent, what the hell do you do with the reams and reams of material your clients submit to you? First of all you're going to be much too hung over from lunch to read anything and secondly why ruin what could be a perfectly nice day reading stuff you couldn't give a damn about. So here is ingredient number four. Be sure to hire a smart, ambitious assistant. Since you're not going to read or submit any of the crap that comes in, make sure you have an assistant who will not only read some of the scripts but every now and then submit one or two to whomever an agent is supposed to submit them to. This will be the only possible way a writer's script has any chance of getting into the right hands. You don't have to know to who, to where, or how he or she does it. That's their problem. If they can't handle this simple task they have no business being in the business. Now should you not have a smart, ambitious assistant but one that is drop dead gorgeous and who you're banging, well, then that's the writer's tough luck, isn't it? He's just screwed and that's that. It's one of the pitfalls of the creative field and writers need to grow up and face the world as it is, not as they'd like it to be. There is one last thing. This is not so much an ingredient as it is one of the sad realities of this precarious profession. Above all remember, a writer is the most ungrateful, unappreciative, thankless bastard on the face of the earth. There is no way you can ever make him happy and inevitably he's going to leave you and get another agent. So how do you handle that? Very simply. You say fuck those little paranoid ingrates. You've worked your ass off long enough for them and if they can't see it, then they're the ones with the problem.

(Looks at watch.)

Oh, my.

(to audience)

Lunch!

Information on this playwright may be found at:
www.smithandkraus.com.
Click on the AUTHORS tab.

White Fire/Black Fire
Alana Ruben Free

Seriocomic
Rembrandt, forties to fifties

Rembrandt emerges from behind his self-portrait at the Metropolitan Museum and talks to a young woman named Eden who is holding a journal and a pencil trying to sketch.

REMBRANDT: Go into the conflict within yourself, and put that into your work. My self-portraits reveal all anyone will ever need to know about me: The pain of my dead children, dead wives, fickle patrons.

> *(beat)*

Give yourself credit for falling in love, marrying, mothering, divorcing, falling in love again. You must write about life how you see it, not how others wish you saw it. That is the artist's prerogative. Honesty is a burden. It is easier to lie, but I couldn't and you can't. If he was stern, I painted him stern. Write about what you love. Love who you love. And don't make any apologies. Try some self-portraits. It might help you see yourself with more compassion. Can you sit with the terror of the unknown? Can you endure loneliness? Can you let my energy into you? You are a masterpiece! A complex masterpiece! Your life, as Eden Simon, is so short, why waste it fighting who you are. It's the same struggle for every Jew I know: To let go or to hold on. I lived amongst the Jews in Amsterdam. I spent a lot of time observing the "New Christians" from Portugal trying to return to Judaism. Observing them, I realized that suffering does strange things to people, and so does hiding who you really are. There is no greater pain than to pretend to be something that you're not. It puts the soul in pain, and we often do to ourselves what was once done to us, only worse. We each have our own unique path out of our own unique suffering. Not everyone can be religious and not everyone can be secular. Vermeer lusted after the Milk Maid, I desired Susannah: Two lusty men, lusting in very different directions. This museum would be awfully boring if we all wanted to paint the exact same woman! Your life is in your hands, but time is in God's. When it's time, you'll know the answer to your question about Demian. Now, kiss me good-bye before the guard turns around. Go home and try a self-portrait . . . naked.

THE WHY OVERHEAD
Adam Szymkowicz

Comic
Nigel, twenties to forties

Nigel shouts to his co-worker Annie who has just left the room. She has unsettled him, but does not seem particularly unsettled herself.

NIGEL: You better run. You better be afraid of me. I am a man. I am a big man and I won't take this kind of insanity from a girl like you! I have scaled mountains. I have forged rivers. I have run in races. I built snow caves and spent the night in them. You hear me?! I jumped out of airplanes. I drove a motorcycle. I am very hairy. I work out two or three times a week. With free weights. I eat lots of vegetables. I am a fairly good pool player. Also pinochle. I could catch a tiger if I had the right equipment and enough time on my hands and if I was in the vicinity of tigers. I have a charming personality. I can make up jokes that people repeat later and don't even realize they're mine. I can make intricate cages out of popsicle sticks. My chest is enormous! I am a wealth of knowledge about music and musicians, especially in the years nineteen fifty nine to nineteen ninety-four. I write poetry. I won an award once for punctuality. My smile is terrific. I used to be a choir boy. I can peel oranges with great speed and dexterity. I am good at choosing shoes. I once played tennis for three hours. I am omnipotent! Okay, well maybe that last one isn't true. But I am a man and I will crush you. You hear me?! YOU HEAR ME?!!

Information on this playwright may be found at:
www.smithandkraus.com.
Click on the AUTHORS tab.

Comic
Donald, twenties to forties

Donald tells his plans to his formerly alive, now deceased taxidermied cat, Mittens.

DONALD: Mittens? I finished it finally. My manifesto. You want to hear it? Oh good. I was hoping you'd want to hear it. Are you ready? Are you comfortable? "Manifesto to leave behind after everything has happened to explain why in case it is less than obvious." Is that title too long? Yeah I don't think so either.

(DONALD clears his throat.)

"There are certain times in history when certain actions become necessary. Right now it is a time when there are great inequalities. I have taken on the responsibility to right wrongs to stop injustice and to use the pen here and later the sword so that the words from my pen will be read. Anyone can write anything, but you also have to get people to read what you write. That's what the sword is for. I stand before you a man ready to take drastic actions. There are men that take actions and men that do nothing but complain. We are all angry but only the brave few who stand up and fight back will be able to accomplish anything of note. History will show that my actions were the right actions at the right time. History will record today as the turning point for America when a wave of citizens led by me took back their country."

"I ask that in my absence, one of my future followers take care of my cat Mittens. She needs neither food nor water. She has evolved beyond life. She only requires company and for someone to talk to her and listen to her. I know that Mittens and I will see each other in the next life and I wouldn't be surprised if she became a conduit for my messages from beyond the grave. In the past, I have spoken to many great leaders through her. Like Marie Antoinette, John Adams, Martin Van Buren, Henry Ford, and a spirit guide dog named Hamish. So when you need to reach me, ask Mittens nicely and I'm sure she will oblige. And through her I will give you future guidance on how to overthrow the government and corporations and create a civilization for the people by the people. The right people, that is."

"In conclusion, when statues of me are built, I ask that Mittens be portrayed as well in bronze or gold or whatever. Her guidance has been incredibly helpful and without her I couldn't have accomplished what my actions accomplished. Like the straw that breaks the camel's back, the small deeds of today will reverberate for generations."

"I sign this with my left hand though I am right handed." And then I signed it. Do you like it?

Information on this playwright may be found at:
www.smithandkraus.com.
Click on the AUTHORS tab.

Comic
Gil, African American, forty

Gil is still a struggling actor at age 40. Here, he is talking to the audience about his church-going mother, Adelaide.

GIL: As a matter of fact, the last time I was in a church it was very upsetting! We hadn't been to church in a really long time and Adelaide, my mother, said to me one Sunday morning that we had to "get up and get us some Jesus!" "Get us some Jesus?" I thought, as a precocious ten year old, I thought that Jesus had moved or something by the way that she had been throwing parties and cussin'! You see, the Saturday night before we went to this church service, we had a rent party. Why? Cause we needed the rent. Adelaide and my Aunt Glo made covered plates which I served for $5. I was my mother's maitre'd-slash-slave. Everyone was smoking and drinking and carrying on. Well, Adelaide was nowhere to be found until her latest boyfriend, Ray Ray, was caught showing some woman the backyard and stayed out there a little too long. My mother leapt out into that backyard as if she was that Bruce Lee doll with the Kung Fu Kick! You remember those? How old are you? Never mind! My mother cussed and turned that party OUT! I handed out coats from the bedroom with exceptional velocity! Adelaide went to bed drunk and shattered as I cleaned the entire house and sampled all of the left over cocktails. So when Adelaide yelled into my room first thing Sunday morning, that we were going to get up and get us some Jesus, I thought, was this heifa crazy??? I was trying to get up and get us some sleep!

Comic
Mo, African American, forty

Mo, a flamboyant gay man, is driving with his friend Gil to scatter Gil's mother's ashes in Disney World.

MO: The last time I was up and around here, I spent time with my baby cousin Khanundrum. Yes, Khanundrum, the "h" is silent! I was reading her a story about Winnie the Poo and lo and behold the story just kept revealing to me, that Winnie the Poo—Poo was a BIG OLD PIGGY BOTTOM! Seriously! What bear runs around with no pants on? Always running into the woods with his "friends" in search of honey? Horrifying!!! So, I started to read all of the children's books that was in the nursery to Khanundrum! *Snow White and the Seven Dwarves*! All about some evil queen that is angry that someone is fairer than you. Hmph! *Goldilocks and the Three Bears*! Just breaking and entering! Those bears should have wore that ass out for eating up their shit, breaking their chair and sleeping in their beds! And the fairytale queen herself! *Cinderella!* Another story about a white woman in distress! But what? Her foot is the only foot that fits that glass Jimmy Choo and what? BAM! She is a princess and gets to marry the hot-ass prince charming! Hmph! But that only happens to White princesses. Tiana has to work her ass off. Trying to open another Cajun restaurant in the South! Making beniets and turning into a frog and whatnot.

BETHANY © 2012 by Laura Marks. Reprinted by permission of Jessica Amato, The Gersh Agency. For performance rights, contact Dramatists Play Service, 440 Park Ave. S., New York, NY 10016 (www.dramatists.com) (212-683-8960).

BLACKTOP SKY © by Christina Anderson. Reprinted by permission of Bruce Ostler, Bret Adams Ltd. For performance rights, contact Bruce Ostler (bostler@bretadamsltd.net).

BOB: A LIFE IN FIVE ACTS © 2012 by Peter Sinn Nachtrieb. Reprinted by permission of Mark Orsini, Bret Adams Ltd. For performance rights, contact Dramatists Play Service, 440 Park Ave. S., New York, NY 10016 (www.dramatists. com) (212-683-8960).

CHECKERS © 2012 by Douglas McGrath. Reprinted by permission of Douglas McGrath. For performance rights, contact Dramatists Play Service, 440 Park Ave. S., New York, NY 10016 (www.dramatists.com) (212-683-8960).

THE CHEKHOV DREAMS © 2013 by John McKinney. Reprinted by permission of John McKinney. For performance rights, contact Lawrence Harbison (LHarbison1@nyc.rr.com)

CLOWN BAR © 2013 by Adam Szymkowicz. Reprinted by permission of Seth Glewen, The Gersh Agency. For performance rights, contact Seth Glewen (sglewen@gershny.com).

CONSTRUCTION OF THE HUMAN HEART © 2012 by Ross Mueller. Reprinted by permission of Beth Blickers, Abrams Artists. For performance rights, contact Dramatists Play Service, 440 Park Ave. S., New York, NY 10016 (www. dramatists.com) (212-683-8960).

COURT-MARTIAL AT FORT DEVENS © 2007 by Jeffrey Sweet. Reprinted by permission of Brendan Conheady, Playscripts, Inc. For performance rights, contact Playscripts, Inc., www.playscripts.com, 866-639-7529.

CRASHING THE PARTY © 2012 by Josh Tobiessen. Reprinted by permission of Beth Blickers, Abrams Artists. For performance rights, contact Beth Blickers (beth.blickers@ abramsartny.com).

CROSSING THE LINE © 2013 by J. Thalia Cunningham. Reprinted by permission of J. Thalia Cunningham. For performance rights, contact Lawrence Harbison (LHarbison1@nyc.rr.com)

HONKY © 2013 by Greg Kalleres. Reprinted by permission of Greg Kalleres. For performance rights, contact Ron Gwiazda, Abrams Artists Agency (ron.gwiazda@abramsartny.com)

HOUSEBREAKING © 2012 by Jakob Holder. Reprinted by permission of Quinn Corbin, The Gersh Agency. For performance rights, contact Dramatists Play Service, 440 Park Ave. S., New York, NY 10016 (www.dramatists.com) (212-683-8960).

HOUSE OF THE RISING SON © 2012 by Tom Jacobson. Reprinted by permission of Tom Jacobson. For performance rights, contact Broadway Play Publishing, 212-772-8334, www.broadwayplaypubl.com.

HOW TO GET INTO BUILDINGS © 2013 by Trish Harnetiaux. Reprinted by permission of Antje Oegel, AO International. For performance rights, contact Antje Oegel (aoegel@aoegelinternational.com).

HURRICANE © 2010 by Nilo Cruz. Reprinted by permission of Peregrine Whittlesey. For performance rights, contact Peregrine Whittlesey (pwwagy@aol.com).

IF YOU START A FIRE (BE PREPARED TO BURN) © 2012 by Kevin Kautzman. Reprinted by permission of Max Grossman, Abrams Artists. For performance rights, contact Max Grossman (max.grossman@abramsartny.com).

IT IS DONE © 2011 by Alex Goldberg. Reprinted by permission of Alex Goldberg. For performance rights, contact Alex Goldberg (alexstephengoldberg@gmail.com).

JESUS IN INDIA © 2012 by Lloyd Suh. Reprinted by permission of Beth Blickers, Abrams Artists. For performance rights, contact Beth Blickers (beth.blickers@abramsartny.com).

JIHAD JONES AND THE KALASHNIKOV BABES © 2011 by Yussef El Guindi. Reprinted by permission of Morgan Jenness, Abrams Artists. For performance rights, contact Morgan Jenness (morgan.jenness@abramsartny.com).

LIFELINE © 2012 by Frank Tangredi. Reprinted by permission of Frank Tangredi. For performance rights, contact Frank Tangredi (franktangredi@hotmail.com).